TRANSFORM YOUR COMPANY

ALEX VOROBIEFF

Sussex Way

Published by Sussex Way
Copyright © 2017 by Alex Vorobieff
All rights reserved.

Sussex Way
220 Newport Center Drive, #11-149
Newport Beach, CA 92660
E-mail: admin@vorobieff.com

Limit of Liability/Disclaimer of Warranty:

Publishing and editorial team:
Author Bridge Media, www.AuthorBridgeMedia.com
Project Manager and Editorial Director: Helen Chang
Editor: Katherine MacKenett
Publishing Manager: Laurie Aranda
Publishing Assistant: Iris Sasing

Library of Congress Control Number: 2017902995
ISBN: 978-0-9987581-0-7 -- softcover
978-0-9987581-1-4 -- hardcover
978-0-9987581-2-1 -- ebook
978-0-9987581-3-8 -- audiobook

Ordering Information:

Quantity sales. Special discounts are available on quantity purchases by corporations, associations, and others. For details, contact the publisher at the address above.

Printed in the United States of America

DEDICATION

To all the spouses
who endure their partners' daily frustration
with a dysfunctional business.

CONTENTS

ACKNOWLEDGMENTS

I would like to thank my wife, Christine, for enduring my frustration when I was stuck, and for her unwavering support and love (which I have tested, a lot).

Thank you to my daughter, Kate, who asked the essential questions: "Dad, are you frustrated?" and "Why are you honking at everyone?"

I am grateful to my dad, who showed me how to slow down and enjoy life with books, walks, and a nice conversation; to my mom, who believed I could do anything—I miss you; and to my grandmother, whose own book inspired me to write my own.

Thank you to Mark and Pat Lee—the best in-laws anyone could ever have—for everything (and for putting up with me).

Katherine MacKenett, Jenny Shipley, Helen Chang, and the team at Author Bridge Media, I could not have written this book without your help. Thank you.

I am grateful to my 3Unitas colleagues, David Chavez, Amit Kothari, Robin Osborn, Keyne Petkovic, and Rony Zagursky, who provided inspiration, feedback, and support during this process. I would also like to thank David Chavez for encouraging me to explore all the different systems out there instead of focusing on just one, which led to writing this book.

Thank you to Ray Damiano, Dave Weiss, Keyne Petkovic, and my wife for reading the painful drafts and providing feedback and support during this project.

I am so grateful for my friends, colleagues, and mentors, who often blur the lines between those categories and whose influence has helped me learn and grow: Steve Busch, Brad Caban, Freddy Carbajal, Ray Damiano, Peter Dopulos, Andy Gennuso, Luis Faura, Jim Foote, Tom Hardesty, Terry Harris, Denny Hathaway, Eddie Hsieh, Mindy Kaplan, Steve Kenninger, Mark Lee, Jeff Lenning, John McNeil, Peter Montoya, George Pappas, David Savlowitz, Alex Schurawel, John Surge, Roger Wadell, Howard Wang, Ron White, Don Woods, and Rony Zagursky.

And finally, thank you to Anantray "AJ" Sanathara, who knows the rest of the story. Thanks for the early hours, late nights, and positive energy. Lock it up.

INTRODUCTION

The Circle of Frustration

"Why is it so difficult?"

After years of listening to frustrated business owners lament the difficulties of running a business, I noticed something: they were sitting on a country music gold mine.

Only instead of singing about lost love, broken pickup trucks, and warm beer, the frustrated business owner sings about horrible meetings, email hell, and fighting fires all day, every day.

Sound familiar?

You hear about how running a business is supposed to feel. It's supposed to be engaging. You're supposed to see growth every year. The business is supposed to give you the freedom to live life on your terms.

But your reality is different.

You feel like you are stuck and going around in circles.

You go through repeated cycles. In each cycle, your frustration level spikes as you wrestle with the same problems. And those problems only seem to be getting worse over time.

You've tried to fix them. Maybe you've hired people with "big company" experience. Maybe you've implemented some business ideas from the popular books you've read. Or you've tried new software systems and consultants who promised to fix everything, hoping to get control of the chaos, but none of them worked. Heck, some of them even threw gas on the fire.

On paper, all these ideas should help. But when you apply them, they fail—and you don't know why.

Is your business different? Are you just beyond help? You want to stop fighting fires and prevent them from ever starting in the first place, but you don't know where to start.

So you go back to doing what you've been doing: the same thing, over and over—and it doesn't get better or easier. If anything, you feel like you need to work harder to keep your head above water. You sense you are just paddling in a circle of frustration.

And all this negativity isn't quarantined to your business.

It spills over into the rest of your life. It hijacks your mind and appears in not-so-subtle nightmares. Your friends and family keep asking what is wrong or, worse, have stopped asking. You yourself might be flirting with emotional bankruptcy. You're searching for a way out—anything that will improve this situation. But you don't have the strength for another false start.

You want to transform the business and make it what you've always envisioned. But to do that, you need a path that will get rid of this frustration once and for all. You need a logical way to move forward.

You need a place to start.

Start at the (Real) Beginning

Transforming your business begins with finding the unique starting lines for you and your organization.

In today's business lexicon, we put a lot of focus on the finish line. Most business concepts are designed and marketed as express lanes to the end goal. However, they make one critical error.

They assume that where you start is not relevant.

When you know your personal starting line, you can finally reach the finish line: a business where everyone is on the same page, asking great questions, confronting reality, and making the best timely decisions to gain an advantage over the competition.

When that happens, the question "Why is it so difficult?" stops playing in your head every day.

The frustration disappears, and a feeling of satisfaction replaces it. Your business transforms from an energy drainer to an energizer. You begin to strive forward instead of in circles. Constant worry stops gnawing at you. Instead of dreading the daily grind, you go into the office every day looking forward to making your business even better.

The rest of your life improves, too. You can take a

vacation with your family and actually enjoy yourself while you're away. Better yet, when you return, you can open your email without that familiar feeling of dread, bracing yourself to deal with the fires that have raged in your absence.

When people are on the same page, the fires stop, and the perpetual state of crisis in your organization vanishes. In their place, you have important answers and clear lines that align decisions and action. Your team knows how to use the right questions and answers to diagnose problems, address them, and keep moving forward.

You finally have a business that works for you. And the confidence to grow it.

Unclogging the Sewer

How do I know all this?

Well, the short answer is, I bring clarity to chaos.

I started my career working as an accountant and consultant for Kenneth Leventhal & Co. when it was acquired by Ernst & Young. We worked on cleaning up financial messes. After I earned my CPA and left Ernst & Young, I moved on to dealing with the financial and information chaos of many dysfunctional companies, which I also cleaned up.

I referred to what I cleaned up as the "accounting sewer," because every decision a company makes inevitably flows into the numbers. To me, cleaning up the accounting sewer was a fun, rational puzzle—a way to bring order to chaos.

But I soon found that cleaning up the numbers was the easy part.

It wasn't long before exasperated business owners started asking me, "Hey, you cleaned up the numbers . . . do you think you could help me take my company to the next level?" And that was when the trouble started. Once I crossed over the numbers line, I got sucked into the emotional frustrations of the businesses—the symptoms of horrible meetings, email battles, and the never-ending fires.

I knew that the accounting sewer was a symptom of dysfunctional companies. But what was the root cause?

I became determined to figure this out. Slowly, I started to notice patterns among the dysfunctional companies that were frustrating for people to work in or with. Nobody was on the same page. It was never clear who was responsible for what, what the company was trying to accomplish, or what was essential for the company to be successful. There were also a lot of unanswered questions, which manifested as conflict in meetings and emails or resignation that nothing would ever change.

Meanwhile, when I worked with companies where people *were* on the same page, those organizations were more than just surviving. They were aligned and thriving.

This insight excited me. *Can you align a company?* I wondered. *Would that remove the cause of the dysfunction?*

I spent years figuring out what it meant to truly "align" a business. But when I finally got it, the results spoke for themselves. Dysfunction lifted. Companies that used to be stuck started to strive.

Alignment changed everything.

It can change your business—and your life—too.

Bringing Clarity to Chaos

As I said, for more than two decades, I've worked to bring clarity to chaos for pretty much any type of business you can imagine, from buttoned-down aerospace manufacturers to hip retailers "dropping" the latest Kanye West shoe: public companies and private companies, big organizations and small ones, real estate developers, food product innovators, service providers, builders, retailers, and manufacturers.

I don't specialize in an industry, but in a state of mind—namely, the mind of frustrated business owners and leaders, helping them to get people on the same page so that it is easier to confront reality and make the best possible decisions.

When it comes to gaining alignment, finding the right place to start for your situation is as important as the destination. And I intend to help you do exactly that.

The Process

This book is designed to be your planning guide for a mountain-climbing journey—one that leads out of a valley to the summit of a healthy, thriving business.

You've got to plan and prepare for the trip before you leave. Then you've got to get your team ready. Before you start the climb, you will need to find your starting lines and make some key decisions. Then, after you start climbing, you will be better prepared for the uncomfortable things that may occur.

This book can be the guide you need to make this journey. It shares what is likely to go wrong when you start to make changes, and how to keep those issues from stopping your ascent. It can help you avoid problems before you leave base camp, while you're going up, and even after you've reached the summit—where you will be exposed to different winds that want to push you back down the mountain.

Read these chapters from start to finish first. See if you recognize the critical issues that are keeping you stuck. Then keep the book in your backpack as you begin the climb so that you can refer to it when you need it.

Keep in mind that, like climbing a mountain, aligning your business is a process. This is not a book you can read today, get excited about, and then go and completely implement in the next team meeting. You can't skip steps. It takes time to reflect, ask the right questions, and address the critical issues before you'll be ready to share it with other people.

What you can do is begin the alignment process in your own mind, right now.

Plot Your Course

Tom Petty wrote the great lyric "I'm taking control of my life now. Right now."

So many frustrated business owners and leaders feel like they lack control of their businesses. When you understand business alignment, you no longer have to be one of them.

You can do this. It's not going to be easy or a straight line. But if you take the principles of business alignment and apply them, you can move toward your ultimate goal with as few detours as possible. When the obstacles inevitably appear, you'll have the tools you need to confront reality and make course corrections. And in the end, you'll reach your destination by the most direct possible route.

You can take control of your business and your life. You can transform your company.

It all begins with finding the first starting line.

Let's go.

Chapter 1

The Missing Business School Subject

The Canoe Revelation

My wife and daughter needed a break from the frustration oozing out of me, so they went into the Disneyland Haunted Mansion. I stayed behind by the railing overlooking the river to finish my coffee. One of my clients was stuck in what I like to call the "circle of frustration," and my mind was struggling to figure out the root cause of the problem—and a solution to it—for him.

As I gazed at the river, I noticed a canoe-ride boat pull away from the dock. The leader—a Disney guide dressed in frontier clothes—paddled hard to get the canoe moving forward. Some of the guests in the boat behind him barely paddled, other more eager guests paddled hard, and still others just sat there. It reminded me of my client's situation. *How long can the leader paddle that hard while most people in the boat don't really know what to do?* I thought.

But the guide only pulled the canoe clear of the dock. Then he stood up, faced the new crew, and set out to transform this group of strangers into a team.

After introducing himself, he raised his "fun stick" (paddle). Even though it was second nature to him and obvious to most people, he demonstrated how to hold it and how to use it to propel the boat forward. Then he said there were three rules:

1. Never stop rowing—"If we don't row, we don't go!" He smiled and energetically asked them to repeat it until they got it.

2. No splashing—it used to be blue water ("You don't want this type of water on you; trust me").

3. Don't stand up—only a fool stands in a canoe. "I am a trained fool," he added.

He also explained where they were going and what to expect. Then he introduced his partner in the back of the boat and explained her role: to steer and watch out for other boats.

Wow, look at that, I thought. *Disney did not expect the guests to spontaneously align their efforts. The guide told people what was expected and how to do it before they got going. He didn't assume everyone would know how to hold or use a paddle, or know the invisible lines not to cross. Disney spent some time asking what was important for paddlers to know and how best to communicate it in order to align the riders' efforts.*

With that simple process, in no time, everyone is on the same page.

I considered the contrast that canoe team made with the dysfunctional companies I had been working with for years. If the business leaders I knew were to operate this ride, they would barely say anything to the new people getting in the canoe. They'd just expect them to know the obvious, and if the new people didn't contribute fully, the leaders would just put their heads down and paddle harder to make up for it.

They wouldn't explain ahead of time what kind of behavior was unacceptable. Or they'd wait until after someone stood up to point out that the person had crossed an invisible line. "Why don't people already know not to stand up?" they'd say. "It's so obvious."

That was when it hit me. No wonder these dysfunctional businesses were paddling in circles. They weren't getting people on the same page to align their efforts. Instead, they assumed people would just "get it." The questions of what was essential for people to know so they could work together effectively, along with how and when to communicate it, were not answered. *Bam!*

It was so clear.

When my wife and daughter returned from the Haunted House, they found a different person waiting for them than the one they'd left twenty minutes earlier. "That was some cup of coffee!" we laughed.

I sensed a starting line. And it revolved around this question:

How do we get all the pieces of a business to paddle together?

The Beginning: Business Alignment

I always knew inherently that there was a place to start taking the dysfunction out of a business—and a way to keep it out. The canoe ride gave me a glimpse of the starting line.

The name of that starting line is business alignment.

Business alignment really boils down to a set of essential questions. You as the leader of your company ask these questions about your business. Then you and your team use the answers as reference points to make big and small decisions.

It sounds simple, but business alignment is incredibly powerful. It provides clear but invisible lines and guidance for people throughout the company. Using these lines, people are able to calibrate and coordinate their efforts, so that you can finally get the results you've been expecting.

Alignment always starts from the inner core of a company. In my experience, companies that try to align starting from the outside—where they interact with customers and suppliers—are never able to change.

Business alignment is a logical place to start transforming your company into a business that actually works. It's where you get people on the same page—*before* they start getting frustrated with each other.

The power of business alignment is that it addresses the real cause of the symptoms that make your life hell as the leader of a dysfunctional company—the horrible meetings, the email quagmire wars, fighting fires all day, and so on. Problems like these always come back to people not knowing the essential reference points: where they're going, how to get there, what behavior is acceptable, what is expected of them, and how to get back on course when they get stuck.

Business alignment is the missing business school subject.

We see cover stories of uber-successful entrepreneurs who seem to go painlessly from startup to billionaires in a few years. But those magazines ignore the stories where the excitement wears off, the frustration sets in, and years or decades go by without any forward progress.

How do you transition from you and a couple of people in an open room to tens or hundreds of people who work together effectively? How do you actually get your business to where you want it to go, without everything depending solely on your effort and energy?

It all starts with the question "How do you get people on the same page?"

Not "What planning system do you use?" Not "What is your management system?" But "How do you get people to paddle together in the right direction?"

Business alignment really boils down to the same principle they use at the Disneyland canoe ride: "If we don't row, we don't go." You as a leader are responsible for getting people to effectively row together. And you do that by asking essential questions and then communicating using the answers.

At its core, business alignment helps you find a starting line, so that you can finally plot a successful course to the finish line. And just like any journey, before you take the first step, you need to know where you are and what is standing between you and the destination.

Many of the business leaders I work with start out in a similar situation: moving in a frustrating circle, but with different things keeping them stuck.

Paddling in Circles

Paddling a canoe without aligning the efforts of the people in the boat leads to going in circles. Similarly, running a business without coordinating the efforts of the team leads to the circle of frustration.

The circle of frustration is a state in which you're trying to move your business forward, but instead you keep ending up back where you started—and you don't know why.

The circle of frustration is a horrible workplace plague. It can choke the life out of you. The longer you stay in it, the more the frustration compounds, and the more drained you and others feel. Worse, it goes home with you, because it is impossible to leave it at the office.

You know you're trapped in the circle of frustration when you start hearing the same clichés. These are some I hear most often.

> ***Circular logic.*** "We don't have time to make the business better until things get better." This statement alone can keep a company stuck forever.

> ***Blaming the team.*** "If we had A players, things would be different." When something goes wrong—the business doesn't win an account, or a project gets botched—leaders often fall back on the refrain of "I just need A players." They don't realize that they do get some A players, but those people tend to get frustrated and leave.

> ***BADJ declarative sentences.*** When things don't go according to plan, many leaders stuck in the circle of frustration react with **B**lame, **A**nger, **D**enial, or **J**ustification. They deal with bad news with emotional responses and rarely ask questions to identify the root cause of the problem.

> ***The "next level" delusion.*** "We need to take this company to the next level." The problem with this cliché is that there's no follow-up. No questions such

as "How do we find this next level?" or "What is keeping us on this level?"

An imaginary friend: ART. When I went back through all the leaders I dealt with who were stuck in the circle of frustration, I was struck by how many of them had an imaginary friend named ART— what I call their **A**rbitrary **R**evenue **T**arget. "If we had this amount in sales, things would change, because then we'd be bigger and we could afford better people and more resources. Then, things would be different." ART is the offspring of circular logic.

Ten "number one" priorities. "We just can't get anything done." When you take a closer look, the leaders who make this statement have ten priorities without a clear one to tackle first. Nothing seems to get done except another round trip in the circle of frustration, usually among promises that they "will get to it."

Do any of these signs sound familiar?

Think about your canoe for a second. When you bring people on your boat, push off into the river, and find that things aren't going right, what do you tend to do? Do you dream of a better team or a bigger canoe? Do you question your team's character? Do you get mad at them? Do you paddle harder? Do you decide to wait until things get better to deal with the real issues?

All of this is a drain on your emotional bank account. Until you can get everyone paddling in the same direction, your company is just going to keep going around in circles.

So how do you get off this ride?

Escape the Circle

In my experience, there are three ways to escape the circle of frustration: death, luck, or choice.

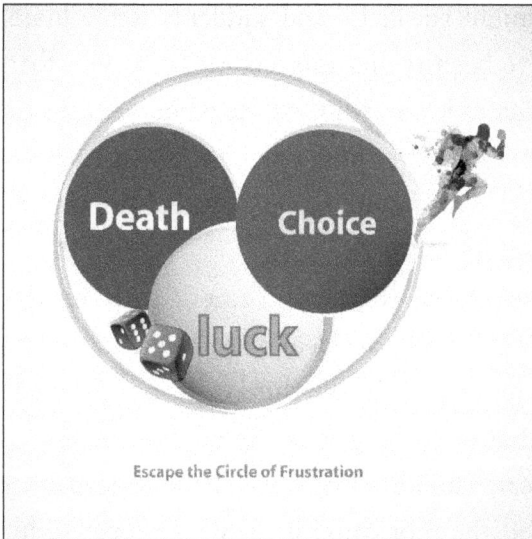

Escape the Circle of Frustration

Death can apply to either the business or its leader. Businesses that stay stuck in the circle of frustration for too long may eventually run out of cash and die. Or the leader can die—literally. If you're continually frustrated and struggling for answers, you can emotionally start to die, and the immune system of the human body can shut down, or a sudden heart attack can strike. Not ideal.

So what are the other two options?

Luck is another exit from the circle of frustration. The problem with luck, however, is that you can't control it.

Sure, some businesses are purchased for large amounts of money, but they tend to be businesses that have something valuable to offer. It's unlikely that a large company is going to buy a business that isn't doing well.

You might get lucky and suddenly win a huge account that you've been trying unsuccessfully to win for years, or hire that great leader who will help you get over the hump. But what if you never find a savior?

Do you really want to wait around hoping for luck to happen—if it ever does?

Probably not. Repeated success with luck is highly unlikely. Luck is not an ideal option, either.

Which brings us to the third exit from the circle of frustration: choice.

You can choose to exit the circle. You can choose to understand the root cause of why you got here in the first place. You can choose a method to get your business moving forward that actually works for you.

But you can do that only if you're willing to take on

the challenge of business alignment by transforming your business from the inside out.

That's what the rest of this book is about: exiting the circle of frustration by choice.

The Path Forward

Before you can choose a tool to exit the circle of frustration, you need a clear grasp of how alignment works.

The heart of business alignment involves asking essential questions, making decisions in alignment with those answers, and repeating the process as necessary. Without asking the right questions, you'll be stumbling around in the dark, blindly following systems that might work for someone else's situation but aren't a good fit for yours.

> The heart of business alignment involves asking essential questions, making decisions in alignment with those answers, and repeating the process as necessary.

These chapters are designed to show you the fundamentals of what alignment is, guide you through the process of assessing where you and your business currently stand, and break down a series of tools that are built to meet you exactly where you are. From start to finish, this is a seven-part process that begins with feedback and ends with leveraging the benefits of alignment.

Confront reality. When it comes to finding starting lines, the first one is inside of you—namely, the six inches between your ears. The one broken circuit that keeps companies stuck is an inability to confront reality. Until that is addressed by fixing your relationship with feedback, it is impossible to start the alignment process. You can't cross your starting line if you don't know where you're starting from.

Start from the inside. After you cross the starting line of your personal relationship with feedback, you're ready to begin transforming your business from the inside. To do that, you need to understand the fundamental pieces that make up core alignment tools (sets of important questions that help you get your team on the same page at every level of the company, from the inside out). I'll show you what those pieces are and why they're important to your company.

Know your bolt-on alignment tools. Bolt-on tools are great business ideas, concepts, and software platforms that you can use to strengthen a specific part of your organization. Leaders are bombarded with bolt-ons, but these can actually make things worse if you adopt them before you're ready. I'll break down the major categories of bolt-on tools to help you understand how and when to incorporate them.

Choose your core alignment tool. There are numerous core alignment tools out there—different blueprints for building a business. It's easy to get caught up in other people's success stories about the core alignment tools that worked for them. But if you really understand the tools themselves and how they work, you have a lot more control—and you're better positioned to make change and confront the inevitable challenges. I'll give you the building blocks you need to make an informed decision about the core alignment tool you use to align your business.

Choose your guide. If you're lost and frustrated, having a guide on your side is going to give you a higher chance of successfully transforming your business. But it's important to pick the right person for you. The right guide will give you the support and push you need to accelerate your progress across the starting line—as well as the finish line.

Maintain alignment. Some of the best things in life take work, especially if you want to keep them running at a high level. Once you achieve alignment, the environment will not stay static, and you cannot set it and forget it. I'll show you how to maintain alignment, so you can avoid sliding back into the circle of frustration.

Find the next starting line. Growth never ends. When your business is aligned, you will be able to leverage that alignment to create a real advantage by increasing the pace and quality of your decision-making process. Once you achieve this, you and your business truly thrive.

We're so results oriented in this world that, a lot of the time, we just want to start at the finish line. We don't want to start at the starting line.

We have everything reversed. And it's keeping us from moving forward.

When you understand the core concepts inside business alignment—and the proper sequence for looking at them— you start to see how they build on each other. You can break down any business alignment tool and match its elements to your needs. You can break out of the circle of frustration once and for all—and have the transformed business you always envisioned.

Everything begins with finding that first starting line: your personal relationship with feedback.

Chapter 2

Confront Reality

The Drawer

I had to know. What was the difference?

Frank's team felt they were finally going to break through. More than eighteen months had passed since I had last seen him. Three years earlier, Frank and I had tried to implement a popular alignment system to help him and his company exit the circle of frustration. But it hadn't worked. We had followed the system's prescribed formula. We'd even used a coach trained in the system to lead the implementation process. Still, something had been missing.

That original alignment system had slowly faded away, and Frank's company had remained in the circle of frustration—until now.

Frank and I sat in his office. I had to know what the difference was for him and his organization this time. What could I learn and apply in the future? The team was buzzing with excitement about the new plan. This was the breakthrough they'd all been waiting for.

"So, what's different now?" I asked Frank. "Where did we go wrong the first time? Is this a better system? Do you have a better coach? Tell me what you guys are doing."

Frank paused and thought about how to respond. Unlike his team, he still seemed frustrated and anxious to me. Then he sighed and gestured sadly toward a drawer in his desk. "Alex, I spent $15,000 on this new plan, and it has been sitting in that drawer for more than six weeks. I can't bring myself to read it," he said. "It feels like there's a force preventing me from opening the drawer."

And that was when I understood.

Nothing was different. A plan for confronting reality was sitting in his desk drawer, and Frank was avoiding it. The first starting line was not selecting a method for aligning the company.

The first starting line was in the leader.

Confront Reality

Was Frank unique? When I thought about my different experiences with companies stuck in the circle of frustration, I realized they had a common denominator: there was always some form of *not* confronting reality. This unwillingness to confront reality manifests itself in what I call the leader's unhealthy relationship with feedback.

The first starting line for breaking out of the circle of

frustration for you, as the business owner, is to assess your relationship with feedback.

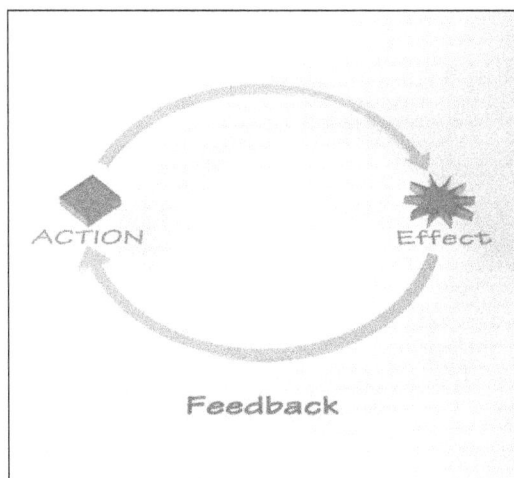

Actions have effects. How you interpret those effects— or the feedback—and change your future actions is how you deal with reality. If you avoid feedback, you don't have all the information you need to make the best decisions.

"It's not what happens to you, but how you react to it that matters." — Epictetus

Leaders with a healthy relationship with feedback are the ones who can objectively confront reality. These leaders are more likely to improve their businesses, because the feedback empowers them to ask truth-seeking questions, objectively assess results, and make decisions that help push the company forward.

Meanwhile, leaders who have an unhealthy relationship with feedback are less likely to change their status quo. Frank had a plan in his drawer to confront reality, but he couldn't look at it. How could it help?

This chapter will help you identify healthy and unhealthy feedback relationships and show you how you can improve your personal relationship with feedback.

Relationships with Feedback

You may be asking yourself, "If a healthy feedback relationship is so important, how can I recognize it? What does it look like?"

The truth is that it is easier to listen for it.

A healthy relationship with feedback exists when you can unemotionally assess the results of your business (also called outputs, feedback, or negative stimuli) and then rationally determine what inputs (or actions) you need to change. It seems simple, and leaders with a healthy relationship with feedback rarely get stuck in the circle of frustration.

Meanwhile, an unhealthy relationship with feedback often shows itself when a leader responds to negative stimuli with negative emotion. The leader's typical response is a BADJ declarative statement—one expressing **B**lame, **A**nger, **D**enial, or **J**ustification. Alternatively, a non-reaction is just as unhealthy. Not responding to something significant is a silent form of denial. Either reaction prevents the leader from confronting reality.

Leaders with a healthy relationship with feedback tend to respond to negative stimuli with objective, truth-seeking questions. Negative emotion does not distract them from finding the real cause of a problem, or from focusing on their desired outcomes. Their attitudes are, "The sooner we confront reality, the sooner we can achieve the outcomes we want."

For either relationship, the key identifier is to listen to the leader's reactions to unexpected feedback. People know how to respond to what they expect will occur, but the unexpected exposes their reality.

Let's look at some examples, to learn how to listen for a healthy or unhealthy relationship with feedback:

Negative stimuli: Losing a key customer

Unhealthy relationship: "They never gave us a fair chance."

Healthy relationship: "Why did we lose the customer? What could we have done differently?"

Negative stimuli: Not hitting a financial target

Unhealthy relationship: "The budget was unrealistic."

Healthy relationship: "What were the key things that did not go according to plan? What will we do differently next time to set targets and achieve them?"

Negative stimuli: Surprise resignation of a key employee

Unhealthy relationship: "We are better off without that person anyway."

Healthy relationship: "Is this isolated, or is this the tip of the iceberg? Why did this person really leave, and why didn't we see it coming? Do we need to change anything?"

Negative stimuli: A missed deadline

Unhealthy relationship: "If I don't do things myself, they never get done."

Healthy relationship: "What went wrong in the process? What needs to be fixed to prevent this in the future? Is this a process or a people issue?"

How do you react when you receive negative feedback? If you find yourself falling into the trap of making BADJ statements or using silence to avoid reality, try stepping back to look at the situation objectively. What questions can you ask to identify the real cause of the problem? What would an objective third party conclude about the situation? What can you and your team learn from it, and how can you make better decisions in the future?

Emotional No-Fly Zones

In addition to BADJ statements, leaders who have poor relationships with feedback often enforce emotional no-fly zones.

In military terms, a no-fly zone is an area where a dominant force can easily shoot down any enemy aircraft that enters it. In the circle of frustration, the leader often enforces his or her own no-fly zone over things that are keeping the company stuck. Nobody wants to talk about the elephants in the room that are protected by the no-fly zone, because they elicit an emotional response from the enforcer or defenders of the status quo.

No-fly zones can take many forms, including untouchables, sacred cows, and unquestionable assumptions.

Untouchables. These are people who are not held accountable or who play by a different set of rules than the rest of the team. When they are in sales, they are usually high performing, but they repeatedly violate the company's core values. When in administration, they have often been there from the start and are intensely loyal to the leader or take care of things the leader doesn't like to deal with.

Untouchables can also be highly compensated family members who don't add value but instead serve to remind non–family members that blood is more important than results. Whatever the form they take, untouchables tend to clash with new people coming into the company, especially those who question how things are done and push for healthy change.

Sacred cows. Sacred cows are subjects that are off limits. People are afraid to question sacred cows for fear of immediate attack. Examples can include underperforming stores, product lines that continue to flounder, or serving markets that produce consistent losses. For some reason—often emotional attachment—the leader believes these items need protection.

Unquestionable assumptions. These are things people have learned not to question, especially in a meeting—even when the conversation prompts questions such as "Why are we trying to compete in three different markets when we show promise in only one?" or "Is our product as good as we think it is?" These questions that seek to confront reality can often lead to the end of the line for the person who questions the unquestionable once too often.

However they show up, emotional no-fly zones hold a company inside the circle of frustration.

In the next few chapters, I will introduce you to a series of tools you can use to align your business from the inside out. The important thing to understand, however, is that every single one of these tools assumes that the leader using them already has a healthy relationship with feedback and does not have emotional no-fly zones.

The worst thing you can do is start aligning your business before you become aware of and repair your unhealthy relationship with feedback. And keep in mind that denial is a very frequent manifestation of an unhealthy relationship. To get the most out of these tools, it's important to honestly evaluate and improve your relationship with feedback *before* you implement them. Otherwise, like Frank, you can spend time and money and still not eliminate the cause of your frustration, or transform your company.

Time to Take Stock

Now that you understand the concept of having a relationship with feedback, you're ready to assess your own relationship.

The key to unlocking the starting gate is getting a triangulated assessment of your relationship. Is it healthy or unhealthy, and to what degree? If you have an unhealthy feedback relationship, you will need to do some work before you can benefit from implementing any business alignment tools. With a verified healthy relationship, however, you have an important key to exit the circle of frustration.

You can use a number of tools to assess your relationship with feedback. These include monitoring your internal dialogue, searching for emotional no-fly zones, looking for missed feedback, and asking others for their perspectives.

Monitor Your Internal Dialogue

The first step in determining your relationship with feedback starts with listening to your internal dialogue. How do you respond when you learn things didn't go according to plan? Do you react emotionally, with BADJ declarative statements, or do you look for the root cause of the problem, using objective, truth-seeking questions?

Write down your internal dialogue, exactly the way it plays in your head. After a week or two, revisit it objectively, as though you were reading a published diary from a historical figure. Do you find emotional statements or truth-seeking questions—especially when you receive unexpected feedback? Does it honestly match the internal dialogue you remember before you started monitoring it?

While you listen for your internal responses, you can search for emotional no-fly zones.

Search for Emotional No-Fly Zones

Do you have any of the emotional no-fly zones mentioned earlier (untouchables, sacred cows, or unquestionable assumptions)?

Again, listen to your internal dialogue during meetings. If it were recorded, what would the transcript look like? Do you fend people off from opening certain issues for discussion? Are people afraid to engage, ask questions, and probe assumptions?

Don't worry if you start to do this and you're a little shocked. It's a good sign if it is easy to determine that you have a poor relationship with feedback, because that is the condition keeping you stuck in the circle of frustration in the first place. By identifying it, you are already improving your relationship with feedback. Seeing the situation accurately is more than half the problem.

The smaller the gap between your self-assessment and reality, the easier it will be to exit the circle of frustration.

Look for Missed Feedback—the Silent Killer

If you aren't finding any feedback to use to judge your reactions, you should be concerned. Feedback always exists, but sometimes it is unspoken. Missed feedback is the silent killer.

Pay attention the next time you propose an idea. Does your team withhold feedback? It's not uncommon for subordinates to avoid giving feedback to someone who has a poor relationship with feedback. It's a survival mechanism.

When customers are boiling angry, many will provide feedback. But have you ever been a disappointed customer and just thought it was easier to find another provider, rather than tell the company what you thought? Or when you were an employee, was it easier to just leave a company rather than say what the boss didn't want to hear?

Once your team becomes more comfortable giving you feedback, you can then take the most difficult step: asking them to describe your relationship with feedback.

Ask Others for Their Perspectives

This is the true test. You have listened internally to assess your relationship with feedback, and you've observed your team's reactions. In a way that encourages candor, you can now ask the people around you how they view your feedback relationship.

First, think about what you expect to hear. When you ask others to describe your relationship with feedback, how do you think they are going to describe it? Could you handle an unexpected description?

Answer the following questions honestly. No excuses or rationalizing it. If people felt they could respond openly, without "hurting your feelings" or burning a bridge with you, how would they answer these questions about you?

- How do you respond when things don't go according to plan: with emotional statements or with questions seeking to find the cause?

- How do you respond when someone tells you something that conflicts with your perspective on an issue?

- Do you have sacred cows or emotional no-fly zones?

- Do people feel comfortable bringing up any legitimate business issue with you?

Now think about whom you will ask. Who can answer and is in the position to state his or her opinion without fear of upsetting you? This may include members of your leadership team, trusted advisors, your former employees, or even your spouse.

It can also be helpful to have an independent third party perform this assessment. This allows participants to respond more honestly, because feedback can be delivered in aggregate.

Again, these answers may be hard to hear. But the bigger the variance between your perception and how others perceive your relationship with feedback, the bigger the anchor keeping you stuck before you even cross the starting line.

And the good news is that once you've done it, now you know. You have started to confront reality by giving yourself an unobstructed view of it. And once you have a healthy relationship with feedback, you can truly start transforming your company.

The points we've just discussed cover the basics of assessing your relationship with feedback. However, there is always more to learn about this key piece of the alignment puzzle. For a more detailed breakdown, you can visit www. BusinessAlignmentTools.com. There, you will find the full feedback relationship spectrum, as well as recommendations for tools you can use to improve your feedback relationship.

Assess Your Team

An organization is generally a reflection of its leader's habits and decisions. That said, once you improve your ability to confront reality, you need to make sure the people around you can as well.

Look at your team and identify which people have unhealthy relationships with feedback. Who makes BADJ statements? Who defends the status quo?

On the other hand, who addresses problems by asking rational questions about the root cause of a problem, rather than reacting with emotion? Which team members seem the most open to learning and growing their skills and capabilities?

It's important to identify both the people who confront reality and the people who avoid it. Those who confront it will support you on the journey ahead, when change gets difficult. Those who avoid it will likely want to stop the process and turn back.

You will need to talk to this latter group before you begin to transform your company. Let them know that you are committed to making this change. You will very likely lose some people during this process. However, keep in mind that you are going to lose either the A players who want to work on an aligned team or the people who are okay with the current environment.

Whom you keep is up to you.

Pull It Together

Because you are the leader, your personal starting position will inevitably be very close to your organization's overall starting position. Once you have verified your starting position and that of your team, you can now start to prepare for the alignment journey ahead.

Based on the assessment process already described, you may have discovered that you have a poor relationship with feedback. Let that sink in. Can you handle that? Or do you want to deny it and put the book down? Things will not get better until you change this relationship.

I had to learn this myself.

I personally used to have an unhealthy relationship with feedback. And ironically, it was Frank who helped me identify it, back when I was working with his company. As

I was stuck in the circle of frustration with him, my own frustration came out in my actions.

After we decided to change our working relationship, Frank gave me some feedback. "Alex, you have a character flaw," he said. He was talking about my tendency to react to problems emotionally.

That was unexpected feedback, and thankfully it really resonated with me. His comment helped me to see reality and develop a healthy relationship with feedback. It literally changed my life.

Once you have a healthy relationship with feedback, you are in the right frame of mind to use business improvement tools and concepts. Your ability to assess the feedback you receive when trying to make changes is critical for success. People will feel comfortable letting you know if your reactions are regressing at the challenging parts of the business alignment journey, and that will help you stay on track.

Cross the Line

Take a good, hard look at yourself and your relationship with feedback. Be honest, and spend some time and consideration figuring out exactly where you are stuck, the position of your team, and, ideally, the current state of the company.

Once you've identified your position on the starting line, congratulations: you've found the personalized starting line to transform your company. And you're ready to cross that line to begin striving forward, using the real alignment tools that best fit your situation.

Now that you have your starting line, you'll be able to select the tools that will finally release you from the circle of frustration. I'll introduce you to the first set of those—core alignment tools—in the next chapter.

Chapter 3

Start from the Inside

From Worst to First

In 1979, the San Francisco 49ers were the worst team in football, with a record of two wins and fourteen losses to their name. By the end of the 1981 season, they had defeated the Cincinnati Bengals to win Super Bowl XVI and were on their way to becoming a powerhouse of modern football.

The turnaround came with the arrival of a new head coach: Bill Walsh. Walsh arrived to lead a team that was in complete disarray on and off the field. Instead of attempting to fix the problem from the outside in, Walsh took a different tactic.

In his words:

"I came to the San Francisco 49ers with an overriding priority and specific goal—to implement what I call the Standard of Performance. It was a way of doing things, a leadership philosophy that has as much to do with core values, principles, and ideals as with blocking, tackling, and passing. . . . Regardless of your specific job, it is vital to our team that you do that job at the highest possible level."

Walsh started the turnaround on the inside of the organization, not the outside where the problems were visible on the field. His Standard of Performance was not limited to players and coaches. It applied to anyone who worked for the team all the way to the people who answered the phones and what they said when they answered the call.

Joe Montana, Walsh's most accomplished player, described his coach's leadership this way: "[It's] his ability . . . to get the whole organization on exactly the same page. On that page he set the standard for how he wanted things done, and his standard was simple."

Walsh created a new core foundation to rebuild the 49ers' entire organization from within. He taught people that if they implemented the Standard of Performance in everything they did, the score would take care of itself. And it did.

In the same way that Bill Walsh transformed the 49ers, you can transform your company by building your own Standard of Performance for the way things are done. And you don't have to reinvent the wheel to build it. There are plenty of systems available to you that make this process easy.

I call them core alignment tools.

What Are Core Alignment Tools?

Core alignment tools are sets of essential questions that help you, as a leader, to transform your business into an unstoppable force from the inside out, using the answers to those questions. The answers, when applied rationally and consistently, lead to better decisions and results.

You can think of core alignment tools as blueprints for building your business, the same way you need blueprints when you build a house. Once you've crossed the first starting line for yourself by embracing a healthy relationship with feedback, you're ready to strive for the next starting line by understanding core alignment tools so you can determine the best system for you.

Core alignment tools start by looking at the inner core of your business and move out toward the perimeter—hence the term "core alignment tools." Starting from the inside is key, because it counteracts the natural tendency for businesses to evolve from the outside, which compounds dysfunction and frustration over time. Core alignment tools are designed to function as the abstract blueprint for your business, giving everyone on the team the necessary insight about what you stand for and what you want to achieve. From there, people can make decisions that align with your company's objectives.

As I said in previous chapters, a healthy relationship

with feedback is critical for any core alignment tool to work. I cannot stress this enough. Every core alignment tool assumes that you are able to confront reality by default. Until you develop a healthy relationship with feedback, you will remain stuck and core alignment tools will not work for you.

> Would you build a house without a set of blueprints? If not, then why would you build something as complex as a business without them?

However, once you are able to confront reality, having the right core alignment tool for your business becomes key to escaping the circle of frustration. To identify the best system for your situation, you need to understand how core alignment tools fundamentally work. This begins with identifying the different pieces of these tools and seeing how they connect to one another.

Core alignment tools are similar in essence once you break them down. This chapter will teach you the components of a core alignment tool by walking you through what I like to call the alignment pyramid.

The Alignment Pyramid

What do core alignment tools boil down to?

Strip it all down, and these tools are a series of fundamental questions that a business needs to ask and answer to get people on the same page. Those answers then foster aligned decisions and actions by people throughout the company, because they all have a common orientation.

Every core alignment tool can be broken down into five levels. My term for these levels is "the alignment pyramid."

The five tiers of the alignment pyramid are core, survival, HumanPower, feedback, and FrontLines. The pyramid starts at the core or inside of the company and moves out toward the perimeter of the business. Each of these is a different aspect of the business that must be in alignment with the others to prevent conflict from arising.

The alignment pyramid is built upside down, and the higher tiers are balanced on the core. Without a healthy relationship with feedback, the pyramid can easily shift out of balance—especially when you focus primarily on the perimeter instead of the core.

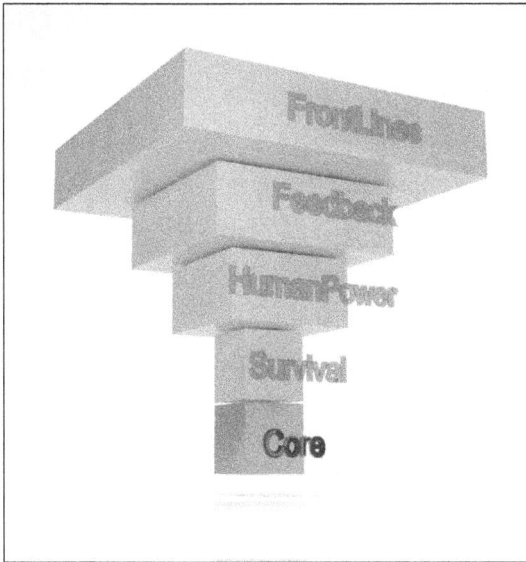

Let's start at the core and work our way up.

Core

Core is the soul of your company. It is the intangible energy that supports and permeates through all the other levels of your business. It even attracts and repels potential employees and customers. The core is the cornerstone of a core alignment tool, and it is located at the base of the alignment pyramid, deep inside the company. For the 49ers, it was Bill Walsh's Standard of Performance.

I chose my first job out of college based on the core of the company that hired me. I had numerous job offers to work for the big six accounting firms, but I chose one that was just outside the top six: Kenneth Leventhal & Co. During the recruiting process, the employees I met had an energy that attracted me. They worked hard and liked to figure things out. They didn't shy away from tackling big client problems. I couldn't put my finger on it, but I knew the company was the right fit. Ironically, many of my classmates were repelled by that same energy.

All core alignment tools define what makes up a company's core differently, but most have some combination of these things: purpose, vision, core values, culture, and mission.

The core is the starting point that defines *why* your company exists and how people are expected to behave. It is the energy that moves your company in the right or wrong direction. A weak core leads to inconsistent decisions and conflict. A strong core improves clarity and direction by acting as the ultimate reference point within a business.

Some examples of the types of core questions that you answer at this level of the pyramid include the following:

- Why does the company exist?

- How do we expect people to behave in our company?

- What are our core values?

- How do we solve big problems?

- What is fundamentally different about how we approach our work? Our industry? The world?

- What big thing are we trying to achieve over the long term?

- What one thought should leaders in the organization always consider when they are making decisions?

- How do we describe our company culture?

There is no one formula for developing the core of a company. It needs to capture and transmit the essence of a living organization to help everyone make big and small decisions.

One sign that a company's core is strong is that, when you ask people in the company what the company's values are, they all describe those values in a similar positive manner. The clearer you are about your core convictions, the easier it will be to attract people who share them.

It takes time to get the components of your core to the point where they can be set in stone. Once set, they should rarely change. They may evolve over time, but these are essential building blocks that are used to determine whom to hire and fire. Making significant changes to the core will likely have a large effect on the people in your organization.

The core is what lies at the heart of a business. The customer inevitably feels it. Left undefined or ignored, it will deteriorate.

How would your employees describe your company's core?

Survival

In the alignment pyramid, "survival" replaces "strategy." Strategy can mean a lot of things, but at the heart of strategy is the question "How is the company going to survive?"

This tier of a core alignment tool deals with what you do, what you sell, to whom you sell it, and how you do it differently that leads to an advantage.

Examples of questions to consider at this level of alignment are the following:

- How does your core influence your survival answers?

- What does success look like for the company? For the business owner, leaders, and team members?

- What things are critical to your success? How are you going to survive and thrive?

- How are you going to make money? What is your business model?

- Who is your core customer?

- How will you attract new customers?

- How does your product or service make your customer's life or job easier?

- What will customers see as different about what you offer them?

- What are you promising customers?

- What are you good at? And how do you do it better than anyone else?

- What is your list of things you don't provide or will not do?

In other words, how are you going to eat?

The business world shares several similarities with nature. Animals in nature use different strategies to eat and survive. We can illustrate the survival level of the pyramid by comparing how rabbits and wolves answer the question "How will we survive?"

Rabbits don't teach their young how to eat. They just go out and forage. Thus, rabbits tend to thrive when things are good in the environment but die out when faced with drought or predators. They don't adapt to changing conditions. They don't confront reality.

Meanwhile, wolves teach their young how to survive using a method that allows them to hunt effectively as a group. Wolves will ostracize members of the pack if they don't hunt within accepted norms. As conditions change, they adapt to reality. They make aligned decisions to survive.

If a company does not have clear answers to survival questions, how will people know what is important? How can they make daily decisions in alignment with their survival answers? On the canoe ride, it was clear: "If we don't row, we don't go."

Your survival answers must be in alignment with your core. For example, if your core is built around breakthrough innovation, you have a serious conflict when your survival methods include "me too" products. When answers to questions are out of alignment, it creates confusion, which generally results in conflict (remember those email battles and horrible meetings?).

Stuck companies rarely spend time deliberately answering survival questions and often end up trying to be all things to all people, willing to do business with them on any terms (rabbit-esque, as well as outside in instead of inside out). This makes businesses complex and difficult to manage and keeps them firmly within the circle of frustration.

Would your leadership team answer survival questions in similar ways?

HumanPower

"Human resources" and "people" do not adequately capture this level of the alignment pyramid. As of this writing, humans still provide the essential brainpower to move companies forward. Why don't we have an equivalent to the "horsepower" measurement of engines?

We do now: HumanPower.

This level of the alignment pyramid revolves around getting and keeping the right people on your canoe so that your company can keep moving in the right direction. In other words, who is on your team, what are they responsible for, and how will the company help them develop and want to stay on the boat?

Bottom line, what is your formula for success with people?

Examples of questions associated with this tier of a core alignment tool include the following:

- How do your core and survival answers influence your HumanPower decisions?

- Why do people want to devote a big part of their lives to this company? Why do they want to work for you?

- How are you going to attract and retain the best you can afford?

- How will you select people? What methods will you use to ensure a high percentage of good hires?

- How will you compensate people (monetarily and emotionally)?

- How will you train them?

- How are you going to grow their skills?

- How will you deal with poor performers? With outperformers?

- What does the organizational structure look like? How does it function? Who can make what decisions?

- How will you increase team effectiveness?

The right people for your canoe must align with your core and with how you plan to survive. Talented people who don't connect with your core will leave. Similarly, you don't need to recruit a bunch of engineers if engineering is not essential for your survival. If engineering is essential for your survival, on the other hand, these questions help define your formula for finding and aligning the right engineers.

When you leave HumanPower questions unanswered, individuals fill the vacuum and companies become dependent on key employees. Vacuums are not always filled in the company's best interest. On the contrary, the vacuum allows fiefdoms and mercenaries to flourish.

Stuck companies spend little time answering the key HumanPower questions, but a lot of time lamenting their lack of "A players." Most often, they hire whomever they can, without a comprehensive program to orient the new hires to understand what is important for the company's survival. The side effect of missing HumanPower answers is that talented, hardworking people get frustrated and leave the company.

Businesses are better able to attract a high percentage of A players when they have clear answers to HumanPower questions—answers that are aligned with a strong core and compelling survival answers.

Look back to the occasions when key employees left your company. Were they frustrated A players?

Feedback

The fourth level of the alignment pyramid, feedback, focuses on determining what is working or not working in your business.

This level is where you start setting specific directions and objectives for the company. It is the feedback loop we discussed earlier: actions produce effects (results), and you decide what future inputs need to change to get the future outputs (desired outcomes) you desire.

Big questions associated with this level of a core alignment tool include the following:

- How do the core, survival, and HumanPower answers influence what things you need to measure and track?

- What are the objectives you are trying to achieve? What do you need to do now to move the company toward achieving long-term objectives?

- What key customer and employee feedback do you need to capture and measure? What tools are necessary to capture and measure it?

- Is the company making money? As much as it planned? Is the company financially healthy? Where is the company generating or losing cash?

- Are you on track to meet your goals?

- What are your key performance indicators? How do people in the company know if they had a good day or a bad day?

- How will you review your progress and adjust course as needed?

The feedback level has more questions than the previous levels because the pyramid is now widening to assess all aspects of the organization. These aspects include financial information, key performance indicators (KPIs), quality measurements, product performance, market information, and customer and employee feedback. Anything that is necessary for leaders to understand reality fits into the feedback tier of the pyramid.

A key part of feedback is measurement. Measurement helps you see reality. Instead of making decisions based on just gut feeling or the last event that occurred, you're able to make rational decisions based on facts. Without measurement, accountability is impossible. How else can you determine whether things are getting better or worse?

Again, one of the big assumptions that all business alignment tools make is that you will make rational, objective decisions. If you don't make rational decisions, the systems will not work. The answers to the questions in the prior three levels will give you some good guidance for what is important and what should be measured.

Stuck companies tend to have broken feedback loops. They do not measure reality and often ignore the negative feedback they receive. At their heart, core alignment tools help you as a company to generate and use feedback, so you can make rational decisions to achieve your objectives.

What type of results or feedback are you trying to generate?

The process of gathering and using feedback also helps to guide the uppermost level of the pyramid: the FrontLines.

FrontLines

The fifth and final level of the alignment pyramid, Front-Lines, focuses on how the business interacts with its customers and the outside world. This is the tactical side and perimeter of the business.

Stuck leaders spend most of their time on the FrontLines. By default, businesses tend to evolve from the FrontLines (outside) and then move inside by adding management (the feedback level) when things on the FrontLines become overwhelming.

Without the benefit of clear and aligned answers for your core, survival, HumanPower, and feedback questions, it feels like nothing is ever right in your business. Disagreements on what is important flare up and frustration spikes. The natural tendency is to try to fix everything that is wrong on the FrontLines before moving inside to the four topics we covered earlier. This is the circular logic of "when things get better (on the FrontLines), then we can work on making the overall business better."

But approaching things from the FrontLines is backwards (outside in). Only once you have moved through the first four levels of the pyramid (inside out) can you answer the final questions to bring your business into alignment.

Examples of FrontLine questions include the following:

- How does our core manifest itself in interactions with customers, suppliers, and other outside parties?

- How do FrontLine employees use the company core to make decisions?

- What processes do we need to deliver value to customers?

- Who is responsible for specific things?

- What and when do we need to deliver to customers?

- What do we do when things don't go according to plan? How do we recover? How do we use the company core to make these critical decisions and take action?

- How do we communicate in regular or irregular conditions?

The FrontLines level is the widest because it encompasses every aspect of how the company deals with the outside world.

Stuck companies struggle with defining who's responsible for what. They're running around as fast as possible—dealing with problems, delivering stuff to the customer, getting unsolicited feedback—but they're not doing it in a cohesive manner, and things slip through the cracks. As a result, you see a lot of finger pointing, because people are not on the same page. People on the FrontLines get frustrated easily because they endure the daily pain of misalignment. This frustration leads to email battles, horrible meetings, and the question "Why is it so difficult?"

When you try to transform your business starting on the FrontLines versus from the inside with your core, the process seems overwhelming, because it is.

Once you start to look at things from the inside out instead of the outside in, however, it's easier to get people on the same page and obtain the outcomes you're looking for on the FrontLines.

Do you spend all your time stuck on the FrontLines?

From the Ground Up

Each level of the alignment pyramid builds on the next. Bill Walsh started the 49er turnaround by implementing a strong core (Standard of Performance). Without a strong core, it doesn't matter how clear you are about how you're going to survive, hire, measure, or execute; your business will eventually come out of alignment on the perimeter and flare up in your inbox and meetings.

But if you're familiar with the alignment blueprint, and you understand how each tier of the pyramid depends on the others to remain strong and balanced, you can transform your company into a force that confronts reality, works through challenges, and strives for new heights of success.

Understanding how core alignment works is an important step for helping your business escape the circle of frustration, and I'll be giving you a breakdown of several specific core alignment tools in chapter 5. But core alignment tools aren't the only resources at your disposal. In the next chapter, I'll show you how you can optimize each level of a core alignment tool for success using focused "bolt-on" alignment tools.

Chapter 4

Know Your Bolt-On
Alignment Tools

From House to Home

As I said earlier, core alignment tools are similar to the blueprints for building a house. They help you define the broad framework and essential elements of your business.

But you can't make the perfect home using that basic blueprint, alone. After the framework is done, you need to optimize the space.

For example, you might survive in that empty framework, but you probably won't be very comfortable without a heating and cooling system. You might also want to enhance your home with good lighting, quality windows, flooring that fits your taste, a security system, solar panels, and so on.

As with every aspect of homes, in business people have developed specific tools to focus on the details of an organization, so that it can not only function, but thrive. I call these systems bolt-on alignment tools.

Bolt-On Alignment Tools

As the saying goes, "Anything you focus on expands." This is especially true in business alignment.

A bolt-on alignment tool allows you to focus on a specific aspect of improving your business. It is not an overall framework or blueprint for organizing an entire business like a core alignment tool, but it works with it to further strengthen the individual levels of the alignment pyramid—your FrontLine execution, feedback processes, HumanPower, survival strategy, and even your core.

Choosing effective bolt-ons for your business and applying them in the correct sequence is essential. If you try to implement bolt-ons before your core alignment tool is selected, you're setting yourself up for failure and most likely wasting time and money. However, when you select the right bolt-ons at the right time, you can help your business to not only survive, but thrive.

After learning more about bolt-ons, you will start to notice them everywhere. Most business books are some form of a bolt-on tool. Bolt-ons are written about in business magazines, presented at business conferences, and used as textbooks in business school courses. They are everywhere, and there are a *lot* of them. Bolt-ons allow you to continually strengthen your business by adding them where and when necessary.

Bolt-on tools fit into the five categories of the alignment

pyramid. Before reading on, make sure you are familiar with the five levels presented in chapter 3. This chapter will then give you an introduction for how and when to add bolt-ons to help your business.

Know Your Bolt-Ons

As I mentioned, bolt-on alignment tools focus on specific areas within the five levels of the alignment pyramid: core, survival, HumanPower, feedback, and FrontLines. And the universe of bolt-ons is constantly expanding. I have included examples here, but I am continually updating the map of this universe of **B**olt-on **A**lignment **T**ools—or what I call the BAT_MAP—as I add new books and concepts. The latest BAT_MAP can be found at www.BusinessAlignmentTools. com.

Core

Bolt-ons at the core level cover in more detail topics such as developing your company's core values, purpose, culture, and vision. They enhance the invisible alignment points that ideally pulsate throughout your business by influencing big and small decisions at every level.

The thinking on these topics has evolved over the last twenty years. Today, tools that focus on core values, purpose, and ideal problem-solving behaviors are the most widespread for developing a strong core.

One of the best bolt-on tools at the core level is Simon Sinek's *Start with Why*.

Start with Why is a great bolt-on for developing a company's purpose. In it, Sinek first dives into the concept of why a company exists. He then goes on to explain that it is critical for everyone to understand and communicate the purpose for the company's existence, because this aligns the company's efforts and connects with customers.

> "The WHY does not come from looking ahead at what you want to achieve and figuring out an appropriate strategy to get there.... Finding WHY is a process of discovery, not invention." —Simon Sinek, *Start with Why*

Sinek goes deep into defining a purpose. This resonates with many people—especially generation Xers and millennials—but it doesn't resonate with everyone. This illustrates the beauty of bolt-ons: you can use the one that resonates with you.

Your core must be your own and resonate with the type of people you want in and around the company. Look around and enjoy the process of developing it, and you can create your lightning in a bottle.

Survival

At the second level, survival, the number of available bolt-on tools grows exponentially. This is where business leaders can easily get overwhelmed without first having a core alignment tool firmly in place.

A big part of survival is strategy. There are numerous strategy frameworks that start with the big picture (e.g., competitive advantage, value proposition, and market position) and drill down to function-level strategy (e.g., marketing, sales, product development, and innovation). Don't get overwhelmed by them. Remember, these concepts just prompt leaders to ask the essential questions that will help them to articulate how to survive.

The book *The Inside Advantage*, by Robert Bloom, lays out one of the best bolt-on survival question frameworks out there. Bloom boils down survival questions to these four:

1. WHO is the core customer most likely to buy your product or service in the quantity required for optimal profit?

2. WHAT is the uncommon offering that your business will own and leverage?

3. HOW is the persuasive strategy that will convince your core customer to buy your uncommon offering versus all competitive offerings?

4. OWN IT!—What are the series of imaginative acts that will celebrate your uncommon offering and make it well known to your core customer?

Sales and marketing bolt-on tools can start in the survival category, asking big-picture questions regarding how the company will successfully sell. Often, they move on to the HumanPower, feedback, and FrontLine levels when discussing specific tactics.

An example is the book *Whale Hunting*, by Tom Searcy and Barbara Weaver Smith, which urges companies to adopt a strategy to avoid responding to requests for proposals (RFPs) and develop a process to build an advantage over the competition to win large contracts.

At this level, bolt-ons should help you hone answers to questions that will help you to survive and thrive.

HumanPower

Bolt-ons in the HumanPower category focus on the process of recruiting, hiring, training, and retaining the best talent to work as effective teams. HumanPower is a rapidly expanding area for bolt-on tools.

One effective HumanPower bolt-on tool is *Topgrading* by Dr. Bradford D. Smart. This book prescribes a structured interview and hiring process to dramatically improve your company's hiring success rate.

Dr. Smart's concept addresses key questions associated with HumanPower: How do we hire the best candidates—people who will be considered a good hire after one year? He notes that, in most companies, less than 25 percent of hires are deemed successful after a year, while the Topgrading methods can increase that success rate above 80 or 90 percent.

A critical part of the *Topgrading* concept is finding candidates who will be a fit with the core of the company, which needs to be defined before trying to optimize hiring.

> "Do not hire a person who does not align with your culture." — Dr. Bradford D. Smart, *Topgrading*

Two more valuable HumanPower bolt-on tools include *The Five Dysfunctions of a Team* by Patrick Lencioni and *Leading Change* by John P. Kotter. *Five Dysfunctions* demonstrates how to get people to start trusting each other so they can deliver results. *Leading Change* discusses how to make real change within organizations.

A company full of A players is the result not of luck but of choice. Choosing the right bolt-on alignment tools can greatly increase your HumanPower.

Feedback

The feedback level is wide and complex. It encompasses not only concepts but entire departments (e.g., accounting, IT, quality, and R&D) and software or platforms (CRM, ERP, etc.), and the number of bolt-ons at the feedback level corresponds to its complexity.

Setting your benchmarks is the natural place to start at the feedback level. First, you need to set the objectives for your business. Then, you want to add the time-specific milestones for achieving them. Determining what and how to measure important items makes it easier to see if the company is on course for achieving desired outcomes.

An example of a widely used bolt-on tool at this level is the SMART objectives system, first used in 1981 by George T. Doran. The SMART formula states that your objectives should be

- *Specific*: target a specific area for improvement.

- *Measurable*: quantify or at least suggest an indicator of progress.

- *Assignable*: specify who will do it.

- *Realistic*: state what results can realistically be achieved, given available resources.

- *Time-related*: specify when the result(s) can be achieved.

Others have continued to evolve SMART objectives over the years, but the concept is the same: it offers a series of questions to better define objectives. You can decide which form is right for you.

With clear answers about what is important to measure, you can shift your attention to the heart of feedback: measuring outcomes to make decisions.

An obvious place to start measuring is with customer satisfaction scores. Is the company doing objectively better or worse from the customer's perspective?

In my experience, stuck companies either have an inflated view of how customers perceive them or judge overall customer satisfaction based on the last customer complaint. The targets are not objective, measurable, and trackable over time.

Technology has changed how customer feedback is measured. Net promoter score (NPS) is an example of a bolt-on tool that seeks to determine customer satisfaction levels with one question: "How likely would you be to recommend the company to a friend?" This bolt-on recognizes that people are now bombarded with survey requests, and if you could ask only one question, this gives a good indication regarding customer satisfaction.

Feedback bolt-ons also include quality systems such as Six Sigma and ISO 9000, platforms such as accounting systems and enterprise systems (ERPs), financial reporting, and the rapidly developing world of key performance indicators

(KPIs). The feedback bolt-on section could be a book in itself and is always evolving. See www.BusinessAlignmentTools. com for a current map.

FrontLines

We have now reached the perimeter of the business. When E-Myth author, Michael Gerber, disparagingly refers to working *in* your business instead of *on* it, the FrontLines are the "in" he was referring to.

However, the FrontLines are also where the magic happens. This is where you align your business from the inside out by deciding what is essential and what will give the company an edge to deliver tangible value to the customer.

FrontLine bolt-ons focus on tactics and techniques for getting things done and delivering what the customer is buying. Strong processes are essential tools for consistent delivery on the FrontLines.

The Checklist Manifesto: How to Get Things Right, by Atul Gawande, is a clear, easy bolt-on that lays out statistical evidence of how different processes, from surgery to commercial flight, benefit from using a checklist. The author breaks down the simple key steps for creating useful tools that help the people on the frontline to make the right decisions and remind them to verify things are done completely before concluding a task is complete.

The business fable *The Goal*, by Eliyahu M. Goldratt, is a

bolt-on that describes one general manager's frustration with getting a factory to ship its finished product to generate cash. The author makes it easy to understand the term "throughput" as the desired outcome in manufacturing and explains how to align decisions and actions toward achieving it.

Once a company is aligned from its core, it can utilize amazing FrontLine tools to improve performance.

Beyond the Blueprint

With an understanding of bolt-on tools, your complete business alignment blueprint is coming into focus. But you can't live in a blueprint. In order to transform your company, you need to build the actual house. Until you start to put the key things into place, your knowledge isn't helping you.

Where do you begin applying these alignment concepts to your business?

In the next chapter, we'll look at which core alignment tool is right for your situation.

Chapter 5

Choose Your Core Alignment Tool

The Best System?

"It sounds like an interesting system, Alex—but is it the *best* system?"

Mike was stuck in the circle of frustration. I had just explained why he should use a business alignment tool called EOS. EOS was one of only two alignment tools I knew of at the time, both of which I had discovered at Vistage presentations.

But was it the *best* system? Mike wanted to know.

I had never actively sought out other options. These types of tools had no name in the business lexicon. What would I enter into the search box?

Mike had a fair question, though. So, I set out on a quest to answer it.

I pulled up the EOS book *Traction: Get a Grip on Your Business* on Amazon and looked at how it was categorized.

The book was listed as a number-one best seller in "Production & Operations" as well as "Organizational Learning." It was also number twenty in the "Management" category. Fortunately, there were also recommendations for related books. I found *Scaling Up*, *Mastering the Rockefeller Habits*, and *The E-Myth*. All were categorized differently, with limited overlap in "Entrepreneurship" or "Management."

After many hours of reading and reviewing these systems, I came to a realization. *These are all tools to help align businesses*, I thought. I did word searches of the different books and saw repeated use of synonyms such as "align," "same page," and "focus."

The systems used different terminology and perspectives, but they all had a similar core: asking essential questions for the different parts of a business, starting from deep inside the company. Many started with a big-picture framework, and some also had more detailed tools. The big differences were for the intended users: Where was the company in its life cycle? What was the mindset of its leaders?

In the end, no one *system* was the best. But I found many great options depending on the specific situation of the company. As the leader of a business, you need to choose the tool that's right for you.

Choose Your Tools

Once you've developed a healthy relationship with feedback as the business leader and understand the elements of core and bolt-on alignment tools, you're ready to choose the tools that are right for you.

What are we talking about when we say "choose your tools"?

You need to know your options. There are a lot of different tools out there, and many people presenting them honestly believe they will work for any situation. However, understanding the differences between them and the ideal situations in which to use each of them makes a huge difference.

Although the options will always continue to evolve, now that you understand the main concepts of core and bolt-on alignment tools, you can identify the best tools to transform your company. We are going to discuss only core alignment tools in this chapter. However, I will give you resources to further research bolt-ons at the end of the discussion.

The best tools for your business will connect with where you are right now—on your personal starting line.

You don't want to waste time and energy trying to implement the wrong core alignment tool. Without investigating your tools before you start, you may get going only to encounter things that feel beyond you or your team's capabilities. You may also lose credibility by choosing a system that doesn't match your company's current reality. At that point, it's easy to lose momentum and end up stuck even deeper in the circle of frustration.

Fortunately, you are now well prepared to choose the tools that best suit your needs.

This chapter breaks down some of the most popular core alignment tools for you to choose from. As you explore your options, select the tool that connects with you and your current situation.

Personalization Factors

More than one core alignment tool can work for a company. The best one for you will fit your company's current needs, its stage of life, your ideal level of detail, the community and resources associated with the tool, and your desired outcome.

Stage of Life

As a business searching for a core alignment tool, you are in one of three S categories: starting out, stuck, or striving. Once you understand your current S category, it makes choosing the right tool a lot easier.

If your organization is starting out, it's a relatively new business. You are in the canoe but not sure of the best way to paddle. You are more willing to change direction to make progress. Often the few people on the boat have limited experience, and they rely heavily on you for everything. Your business model is fluid, and the main question that runs through your mind is "How are we going to survive?"

If your organization is stuck, the thrill is gone. There are more people in the boat at this stage, and you might have multiple boats in different types of businesses. The boat moves forward based on inertia, and assumptions are not often questioned. Changing direction takes a lot of effort.

Deep down, if you're stuck, you know something isn't quite right. Maybe the business will get lucky, but on the current course and pace it is not going to thrive. You might comfort yourself with the thought that the boat is not sinking and wonder if doing something different would really improve things. However, you also wonder if it is worth the risk.

Stuck companies are in the circle of frustration. To get unstuck, you need to choose to exit.

If your organization is striving, it is defined not by its age, but by its momentum and its confidence that it can improve. You wonder how to leverage your momentum and make as much progress as possible. The leadership is willing to question whether the business is on course and is also willing to use the best tools to make progress. You are willing to learn new techniques for paddling more efficiently, and you want to make it easier to bring additional high performers on the boat to help you reach your goals faster.

Most business alignment tools work best for companies that are striving or at least willing to put in the effort to strive. That said, the reality is that most companies that lack alignment are stuck. It is more important to pick a system that does not overwhelm you and that allows you to improve and build momentum. You can graduate to a more sophisticated tool when you are ready.

Level of Detail

The level of detail of a core alignment tool is another important factor to consider. What is your personal preference? Do you like a broad framework? Or do you crave reconciled details and structure?

Some systems are designed for engineer personalities that crave a high level of detail. These are the equivalent of detailed drawings for a house. Other tools provide the broad strokes and architectural rendering of how the house will look and feel. These plans typically don't detail how each part is interconnected. Those broader, high-level plans require more bolt-on tools to fill in the details.

Size of the Community

Some tools are used by a lot of companies. Many of those companies meet on a regular basis to share ideas and best practices. It is sometimes helpful to attend these meetings before choosing a system. Some have a growing group of coaches who can help you. Others have a very small community, because the tool is relatively new or is something one coach developed and implements with his or her own clients. You can decide whether a tool with a large community will be a useful resource for you.

Your Desired Outcome

Finally, when choosing which tool is right for you, the key question is what is your desired outcome? Do you want to build an amazing team to lead for the long term, or are you trying to work your way out of a job? Do you want to create something that you can franchise? Do you want to sell the company? Do you want your leadership team or all of your employees to feel like they have a stake in the outcome?

Part of knowing what you want to accomplish is having an awareness of your ownership philosophy perspective. Are you willing to share information? Are you looking to build a team that can lead and grow the company? In what ways are you willing to take risk to create value in the long term?

At the end of the descriptions of each tool on the following pages, you will find a short checklist that shows which stage of life, level of detail, and desired outcome the option fits. I will also indicate the relative size of the community associated with each, so that you can target your due diligence.

Narrow the Search

By understanding the different attributes of alignment tools, you narrow down the search to find the ones that are the best fit for your current situation. Take a look at the following starting out, stuck, and striving core alignment tools to determine which of them show the most promise for your specific business.

Starting-Out Tools

At the starting-out stage, your business is still forming. You wonder if you are headed in the right direction. You need the right tools, but the business relies on you, every day. You need a blueprint to build a successful business while you are making a living inside it.

Two popular alignment tools for this stage include *The E-Myth* and *Built to Sell*.

The E-Myth

The E-Myth by Michael Gerber focuses on learning how to work *on* your business, not *in* it. It discusses the process of designing a business that is repeatable using the example of Sarah, an owner of a pie shop who is struggling to keep her store open. Once your business model is repeatable, the concept can be leveraged by selling franchises.

Gerber writes, "The true product of a business is the business itself." *The E-Myth* is ideal for a company that is starting up, but it can be used for a small stuck business as well.

- **Stage of Life:** Starting out (primary), small stuck companies (secondary)
- **Level of Detail:** Medium
- **Size of Community:** Relatively small
- **Desired Outcome:** Build a business that is franchisable.

Built to Sell

Built to Sell by John Warrillow assesses whether you have a business you can sell. His concept is to create a business that can thrive and that is valuable without you. You focus your strengths on what is scalable. This book outlines Warrillow's philosophy through the story of one person figuring out what he wants, failing, and ultimately making decisions that allow him to live the life he desires.

- **Stage of Life:** Starting out (primary), small stuck companies (secondary)
- **Level of Detail:** Medium

- **Size of Community:** Medium, with various levels of certifications

- **Desired Outcome:** Build a business that is sellable at a premium, or one you're happy to own that doesn't eat up your life.

Stuck Tools

As I've said before, if you're really stuck and have a poor relationship with feedback, you probably don't want to waste time and money choosing and implementing a core alignment tool yet. A better first move for you may be to find the right business coach (which we'll discuss in the next chapter), who can help you improve your feedback relationship and prepare you for the process of using a core alignment tool. The encouragement and accountability that the right coach offers will help you make real progress faster.

Once you do have a strong relationship with feedback, you'll want a tool that is accessible and digestible for you. Small, successful steps are important to get unstuck so that you can begin moving toward a striving mindset.

Three tools that work well for stuck companies making the first steps toward striving are *The Advantage, Mastering the Rockefeller Habits,* and EOS.

The Advantage

The Advantage by Patrick Lencioni is a tool to diagnose the health of an organization. This book is applicable to all companies, at all stages. At its core are six basic questions whose answers can be used to align an organization toward healthy growth. Use this tool to assess and establish a framework for your business.

Although it is not a detailed "how-to" book, *The Advantage* provides easy-to-follow insight and a path for building a healthy, aligned business. This is a great tool to use to start defining your alignment pyramid.

- **Stage of Life:** Stuck (primary), all (secondary)
- **Level of Detail:** Low (broadest framework)
- **Size of Community:** Limited; no formal network of coaches
- **Desired Outcome:** Make consistent decisions and reinforce the right behaviors to build a healthy, aligned organization that can deliver results.

Mastering the Rockefeller Habits

Mastering the Rockefeller Habits by Verne Harnish identifies ten behaviors of successful businesses. The author infers that John D. Rockefeller exhibited many of these habits, which helped to make him the richest American ever. The book discusses ten relatively simple habits with detailed subhabits. It is ideal for a stuck company because you can take one habit at a time, implement it, and get it right before adding the next habit.

- **Stage of Life:** Stuck (primary), early striving (secondary)
- **Level of Detail:** Medium
- **Size of Community:** Medium; informal network of coaches
- **Desired Outcome:** Implement the habits that will allow for consistent growth.

Entrepreneurial Operating System (EOS)— Traction

EOS is a core alignment tool designed to give a company "traction" toward achieving its goals. The EOS series by Gino Wickman compares running a business to a computer operating system. It has six understandable pieces to get a business to run well. This is an accessible system that builds you up as long as the leader has a healthy relationship with feedback.

- **Stage of Life:** Stuck or striving
- **Level of Detail:** Detailed

- **Size of Community:** Large and growing; formal network of coaches

- **Desired Outcome:** Align your business for long-term growth.

Striving Tools

When your company is striving, it needs to be challenged. The good news if you're at this level is that most core and bolt-on tools are really designed with strivers in mind. At this stage, you are ready for concepts and insights that might require some effort to grasp, and you are willing to struggle for valuable insight.

If you are already striving, you don't want to waste time listening to people explain things that you already know. You've been exposed to a lot of concepts, and you need help pulling them all together.

Two popular alignment tools at the striving level are *Scaling Up* and *The Great Game of Business.*

Scaling Up

This program is the evolution of the original *Rockefeller Habits* by Verne Harnish. It takes the broadly understandable concept from the first book to a higher level of insight and detail. *Scaling Up* needs a detailed striver as a leader more than any other system, and it works best when all of the members of the leadership team want to push themselves to digest and implement a comprehensive blueprint for growth. It is ideal for companies that have already completed the Rockefeller Habits and are looking to increase their momentum.

- **Stage of Life:** Striving

- **Level of Detail:** High

- **Size of Community:** Growing; formal network of US and international coaches; annual conferences to learn about new tools and best practices

- **Desired Outcome:** Build an organization that can successfully grow exponentially.

The Great Game of Business

The Great Game of Business by Jack Stack is the system developed and implemented by a company with no choice but to figure out a way to survive.

In 1983, the Springfield, Missouri, facility of International Harvester was going to be closed. The management team borrowed $11 million to purchase the subsidiary with only $100,000 in equity. There was not a lot of room for anything to go wrong.

Jack Stack, inspired by his high school basketball days, realized that when people know the score, they tend to focus their efforts on achieving results. So he developed a simple program to let the frontline workers know the score and how they were helping the team. They developed three simple principles: teaching the rules of the game, following the game by keeping score, and providing a stake in the outcome.

- **Stage of Life:** Striving
- **Level of Detail:** Medium
- **Size of Community:** Large; US and international, and growing; has an annual gathering every September for companies to share their experiences and learn techniques
- **Desired Outcome:** All levels of your company are engaged with a stake in the outcome.

These are just a few of the core alignment tools available on the market today. For a list of others, you can visit www. BusinessAlignmentTools.com.

Bolt-Ons

All tools discussed on the previous pages are core alignment tools, because it is important to select a core tool before you can successfully install bolt-on tools.

If you are starting out or stuck, the best course is to stick to one core alignment tool until you know it inside and out.

If you work with an experienced coach to implement a core alignment tool, he or she is likely to bring in the right bolt-on tools to enhance that core system as you implement it.

If you are striving, you are better able to see the five levels of the alignment pyramid in your core alignment tool and determine where you want to add bolt-ons. Doing it yourself is more challenging, and working with a coach tends to increase the depth of the discovery process and the quality of the outcome when it comes to bolt-ons. That said, as mentioned previously, I've put together a list of bolt-on tools for you to start to explore on your own. You can access it at www.BusinessAlignmentTools.com.

Growth: Unlimited

Now that you understand how to narrow your focus to find the best core alignment tools for your situation, you are ready to start the selection process. Most people get stuck trying to implement the tools that find them instead of finding the tools that are best for their unique situations. With the understanding you've gained in this chapter, you can start to vet your options from an informed position, so you can choose the one that will successfully transform your company.

But even if you know all there is to know about your options, putting them into action is another story.

The next chapter will show you how to choose the best guide to help you align your business at the ideal pace.

Chapter 6

Choose Your Guide

Up the Mountain

Growing a business feels like climbing a mountain. If you know you are not making progress, that sinking feeling sets in.

I felt that way in 2006, when I was running Certified Aviation Services for one of my clients, who had recently purchased it. Two of our large customers went bankrupt on the same day, and we were experiencing huge losses. I was ready to tear out my hair in frustration. My unhealthy relationship with feedback flared up in a big way. Just ask the office trash can I kicked across the room. I needed some help to transform the company.

I needed a guide.

The guide I found was John McNeil. He opened my mind to the idea of getting results by implementing a system. He shared the tools he used to help companies transform successfully. Then he helped me prepare our team to climb the mountain together.

John was great at asking the right questions, boiling down the responses on the whiteboard, and distilling summaries of our decisions—all of which got us clearly on the same page. We left the first offsite meeting with a workable plan. Even better, he was an objective person who could question our reality blind spots.

He could see we had issues working as a team, and he helped us prepare for hard decisions. Over time, we made progress—slowly at first. Then faster.

By the following year, the company had earned record profits.

The process of working with John opened my mind. When I looked at other clients who were not stuck in the circle of frustration, I saw the correlation. They, too, typically had coaches to help them develop plans, review progress, and realign as necessary.

They didn't try to climb a mountain by themselves.

Transforming your business is a big mountain to climb. Deciding who can help you implement alignment tools is as important as deciding which tools to use.

Your Guide to Growth

You have assessed your relationship with feedback. You have narrowed down the choices for the right core alignment tool. You now have another decision to make: Will you climb this mountain alone, or with a guide?

You can try to do it by yourself. However, the more stuck you are, the more helpful it is to have the right guide. For this reason, most stuck companies do use a guide.

But all guides are not equal.

You shouldn't just hire someone whom you happen to hear speaking, for example. There are different types of coaches and systems out there, each with different styles. You need a guide who understands and can work with where *you* are on your starting line.

If you have chosen your core alignment tool, you've already chosen your method to climb the mountain. Now you can choose a coach who is experienced with your core alignment tool and personal starting line.

If you have the right guide on your journey, he or she can reduce the amount of time you need to climb the mountain. You will not turn back at the first sign of things not going well. An experienced guide has seen what can go wrong and will prepare you to keep striving forward. He or she understands where leaders and teams get stuck. A good guide watches your progress and provides objective feedback, helping you to confront reality.

Without a guide, however, or with the wrong guide, it is all too easy to get lost or give up before reaching the summit.

This chapter breaks down what to look for in a guide, where to look for one, and how to interview potential guides. Just as you discovered the right tools for your situation, you can also find the best guide for your journey once you know what to look for.

The Key to a Great Guide

You want a guide who has experience climbing in the conditions you are facing.

Most of the core alignment tools discussed in chapter 5 have books, specific tools, and people who are certified or trained as coaches in that specific system. There are also independent implementers like John McNeil who have their own systems. The key is finding someone who connects with your frequency and communicates in a manner that you can understand.

The ideal coach is going to drive the implementation process based on your starting line position.

As I've said, most core alignment tools assume that you have a great relationship with feedback, and that you have a team of people around you who are striving to understand new concepts. However, a good coach takes into consideration that you are likely starting out stuck. The right guide doesn't assume that he or she will get you quickly up the mountain because the system is so good it can fix anything, if you just follow the steps. The right guide understands that his or her role is to help the leader develop and use a healthy relationship with feedback to confront obstacles and challenges that come up during the climb.

A good coach will also help you get back on track before you slip over the edge of the mountain, and help you deal with the feelings of doubt that will arise.

A seasoned guide knows the steps to take a new mountaineer up the mountain. He or she knows not to try the most difficult things on the first day, but to set the pace for long-term success. Similarly, an experienced coach will identify what you respond to best. Do you need positive feedback, gentle pushes, and a little room to figure things out? Or do you need confrontation and a kick in the right direction?

I interviewed a growth coach who described herself this way: "I'm either their mother or their mother-effer!" I was surprised to hear that blunt language, but she had a point. She explained that she either nurtures her clients or pushes them "hard as hell," depending on what the client responds to.

A coach is not a consultant. Your guide is not going to do the work for you. The coach's role is to get you to do the thinking so that you can make good decisions yourself. The goal here is to find the coach who is going to successfully work his or her way out of a job.

Let's take a look at how to do that.

Where to Find the Right Coach

Where and how can you start looking for a coach?

If you have narrowed your core alignment tools down to a system or two, you can look to those systems to recommend coaches for you. You are likely to get geographical recommendations. I also suggest going to LinkedIn and searching for the alignment tool you are considering. This will show you active coaches and their professional history.

Be careful with blind referrals, because people will recommend coaches who worked for their situations but who may not necessarily fit yours. Instead, talk to your trusted advisors, such as your Vistage chair or CPA, who know you and the challenges you face. (They may even have been waiting for you to finally ask for help.)

Ideally, you will be able to find two to three coaches who may work for you so that you can choose the best fit. If locating them is difficult, I can help find coaches in your area and screen them for you. You can access this resource at www.BusinessAlignmentTools.com.

How to Choose Your Guide

Once you have a few names and you are ready to start meeting with prospective coaches, the question of how you evaluate them becomes important.

First, you need to check out their toolboxes. Then, you'll want to take note of the questions they ask and how they answer your questions.

Check Out the Toolbox

To get a sense of how much a coach relies on an alignment system, ask what bolt-on tools he or she uses and why. This will provide you with insight into how the coach handles different issues. You want to get behind the coach's presentation and see how the person thinks, and how much he or she has absorbed through trial and error.

If the coach plans to use bolt-ons for your business, find out which ones and why. This brings out the coach's experience and communication skills. Can you follow what this person is saying? Ideally, the coach believes in the core alignment tool but is not over-reliant on it to the point where he or she assumes no outside tools are ever necessary.

If your company is striving, you want to use the best focused tools for strategy, marketing, HumanPower, and FrontLine execution that are available. But if you have a team that is stuck, you want to find a coach who uses bolt-ons sparingly and only when necessary.

Take Note of Questions and Answers

The other key thing when evaluating a coach is seeing that he or she has dealt with the challenges you and your team are likely to face.

Look for the right kind of experience by asking prospective coaches about their past challenging projects. How did they deal with challenges? What did they learn? How have they adapted their styles based on challenges and feedback? How have they evolved their process over the years?

Coaches who don't have experience handling problems remind me of a quote from the captain of the *Titanic*, Edward Smith, in 1907: "I never saw a wreck and never have been wrecked, nor was I ever in any predicament that threatened to end in disaster." The mountain guide who claims to have gone up the mountain fifty times without any issues doesn't have the same experience as a guide who has led fewer but more difficult groups, and who has learned how to better handle those challenges.

Once you have asked your questions, make note of the questions your prospective coaches ask and the statements they make. Do they ask questions to better understand your situation and challenges? Or do they make a lot of statements about how great their systems are and the results you should expect?

Again, these systems do have tremendous benefits and are designed to transform your business, but most are based on the false assumption that leaders using the system are going to make rational decisions using their healthy relationship with feedback. You now know that this is not always the case, so ask them, "What are the biggest challenges that can prevent the successful implementation of this system?" A good guide will want to know as much about you and your team as possible before answering this question.

Be wary if your questions are answered only with how great the system is and how it can solve all your problems. If it starts to sound like the system is unsinkable, it reminds me of another quote from Captain Smith: "I cannot imagine any condition which would cause a ship to founder. I cannot conceive of any vital disaster happening to this vessel. Modern shipbuilding has gone beyond that." We all know how that turned out for the *Titanic*!

The Complete Journey

I saw the benefit of finding the right guide during a visit with my family to Mammoth Mountain Ski Resort.

My six-year-old daughter was so excited to learn to ski. We rented equipment and enrolled her in ski school for beginners. Her instructor walked up—a young man in his late twenties who could best be described as "radical"—and immediately started talking about the techniques of skiing. My daughter's eager demeanor changed, and her lower lip started to quiver. By mid-morning, it was clear something was off. My daughter was becoming scared of the mountain.

She didn't have the right guide.

Even though the instructor knew how to ski and seemed very competent, his style didn't connect with my daughter. So we talked with the ski school and arranged for a different instructor.

In the afternoon, my daughter met her new ski instructor,

a young lady from the local area. She first sought to under-stand my daughter—what she liked, her interests outside of skiing, what she was having trouble with on skis, and how she communicated. They connected first, before the instructor started instructing.

By the time they started to discuss technique, my daughter already trusted her. And within a few hours, they had made big strides and boarded the ski lift with big smiles on their faces.

The right guide can make all the difference. Take the time to select the right one for you.

Once you have selected the best coach with the best tools, you are ready to set out on your journey to transform your company from the inside out. This is where the adventure begins. In the next chapter, I will prepare you for common challenges that arise as you work toward aligning your business.

Chapter 7

Maintain Alignment

Gone Fishing

When I was a kid, my father used to take me sport fishing off the Southern California coast. We fished on open-party boats carrying up to sixty people, who ranged from first-time fishermen to more experienced anglers.

My father and I had mixed luck. Sometimes we got skunked, and occasionally we got lucky and won the jackpot with the biggest fish. Often, we would miss out on catching a really big fish because we were not ready when conditions changed.

On the other hand, we always noticed a few detail-oriented guys who were more successful at fishing than we were.

Over the years, I learned the telltale signs and could recognize who the best fishermen were as we boarded the boat. These people could seamlessly get the right gear in place and their bait in the water, no matter the situation. They watched what was working for catching fish. If they were not getting bites, they tried other methods. If they lost a fish, they identified the reason and addressed it.

The best fishermen were the least excitable and didn't seem to get mad at people. They were humble and focused on what they could control. They didn't need luck to hook a fish. Their demeanor did not change when they caught the most fish. They just kept methodically going through their processes to make sure they were dealing with the changing conditions around them.

My demeanor, on the other hand, did change. After catching a big fish, I usually took a break to enjoy a hamburger. Or I would get angry after losing a fish and miss the opportunity to learn what went wrong.

The fishermen with the best relationship with feedback consistently caught more fish. Time after time, year after year.

This is the ongoing value of maintaining alignment.

Stay in Balance

As a kid learning to fish, you figure out fast that conditions on the water are slippery at best. While growing your business, especially as your feedback relationship changes, it is important to be aware that you are still on a slippery slope.

The business alignment pyramid is inverted for a reason. It doesn't give the illusion of assumed stability. There's an inherent limit to it; you must continually balance it, or it will start to wobble and fall.

To stay in balance, you must make sure that you always look at your business objectively. Maintaining balance can help your team to coordinate and strive to improve what they're doing. When errors in judgment occur, a balanced team can learn from the feedback. Instead of getting over-confident, they stay vigilant—and that helps you land the next big fish.

A balanced business allows you to build on your success and momentum. However, you need to proactively recheck for balance rather than getting stuck waiting for something to break. If you don't pay attention, listen to feedback, and maintain balance, your business will topple and return to the starting line.

You have already started to increase your chances for success by preparing for some common issues on the journey ahead. This chapter further breaks down why we stray out of balance, why you shouldn't "set it and forget it" or let your coach lead for you, and how to keep your business balanced.

The Slide Right Curve

The business alignment pyramid illustrates that stability is not guaranteed, but it is also important to be aware of the Slide Right Curve. The Slide Right Curve says that the results you want will deteriorate over time unless you actively try to improve them, by climbing to the left.

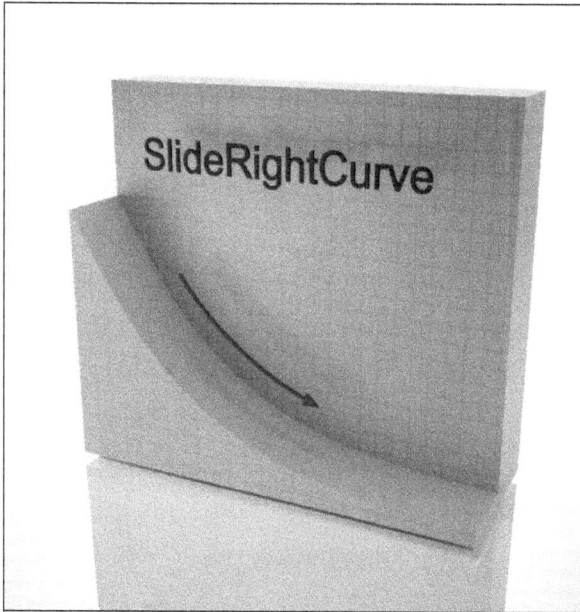

I use marriage to illustrate this concept. You never hear anyone who has been married longer than a couple of years say, "My marriage just keeps getting better and better, and we never have to work at it!" No amount of explicitly stated love can carry a marriage to long-term strength. There will be a natural decline in the marriage unless effort is made to improve it.

The same is true in business alignment. It's important to be cognizant that you are not sliding to the right, and that you are actively climbing to the left, or your whole pyramid starts to wobble.

Don't "Set It and Forget It"

Once you have your business aligned, you may be tempted to think, "I did it! It's done. Now I can cross that off the list and move on to the next thing." That kind of thinking is a trap.

You want to avoid the mindset of "set it and forget it."

I worked with a valve company that landed a big contract with an important client after three long years of trying to win the business. Within a year, this client—a large multinational company—made up more than half the valve company's business and led to significant growth. At first, the valve company made sure everything was on time, asked for feedback, and made the long trips to visit the customer to make sure things were on track.

As time went on, however, the valve company stopped checking in with its customer. The customer continued to send orders for parts, so the people at the valve company assumed everything was fine.

They set it and forgot it.

A year went by. The people at the valve company finally stopped in to see the customer on a trip while they happened to be in the area. They assumed that everything was still fine.

They were shocked to hear the customer wasn't happy anymore and was ready to pull their business.

The people at the valve company hadn't realized that the relationship with this client had been sliding to the right over time. They had to accept significant reductions in pricing to keep the customer, and this pushed the company into a loss. It took time to get back on track. But they learned a lesson about setting it and forgetting it.

Thinking you can set it, forget it, and move on to the next thing is a recipe for regressing back into dysfunction.

The Coach Is Not the Leader

It's easy to sit back and let the guide you hire do his or her job: guide. But remember, your coach is not a full-time employee. His or her job is to help you get unstuck, to see things that are difficult to self-diagnose, and to help implement alignment tools successfully so you do not need the coach anymore.

You are the leader. Engage, question, and push back if discussions are not producing clear and understandable answers to your essential questions. Do the answers help sketch the desired blueprint of your company? Do they resonate with you? Would you feel comfortable explaining them to someone interviewing to join your leadership team?

When you start this process, assume that you are going

to have to stand up and passionately communicate these concepts. I have seen leadership teams allow the coach to lead them through developing core values, purpose, and a vision, but when the leaders read the results of the work, it doesn't connect with the owner. This can happen if you don't fully engage with the creative process and make sure that each piece of your blueprint captures the spirit of what you want your business to look and feel like.

If there is no life in the ideas, they will die. The answers to your alignment questions should trigger emotional connections in you. They shouldn't be a color-by-numbers project your coach gives you that lacks the individuality and customization that only the insiders can provide.

The coach can also become a target. Some people on your team may grow tired of the energy and emotion required to change the status quo. Some of them really didn't mind things as they were, and they may identify reasons to turn back. These are the people who will pick on any perceived flaws in the system or coach. And the coach will likely make some mistakes. If you show you are committed to the process, however, others on your team will follow your lead. Remember that the circle of frustration has three exits, and we have decided to leave by choice, not through death or luck.

Let your coach know about prior emotional no-fly zones beforehand. This will allow him or her to ask pointed questions that can change the collective mindset around the table quickly. When you can show people that all options are on the table, you confirm with your team that you are all looking for the best ideas to help this company thrive. Before long, the best players on your team will become engaged, working to solve problems. You are likely to see some small successes. Keep pushing, and after the first full year of the journey you will gain momentum and feel completely energized. This improvement will take time to solidify and needs to be interwoven into every aspect of the company.

The Balancing Act

What else can you do to keep your business balanced?

First, schedule time to objectively question whether you are keeping the pyramid aligned. Are you making decisions that are in line with your core at each level? Establish a group of people whose job is to play devil's advocate and assess the alignment. They shouldn't tear people down, but they also shouldn't just provide false confirmation. A question they should ask: If the leadership team's decisions and actions were audited to see if they were in alignment, would an independent assessment confirm the alignment?

This review should be done one to four times per year. You can do it in conjunction with an annual planning session or add it to quarterly meeting agendas. Create openings for people to raise examples of misalignment. The more trouble you have maintaining balance, the more frequently you should assess it.

Second, if frustration starts to return, look at the struggles you're having. If they are fundamental problems, the root cause is likely some sort of misalignment within the pyramid, and it usually starts with the core. Reexamine the answers to your essential questions at each level of the pyramid. Do some answers need to be rethought?

If you are hitting your growth targets and getting good feedback from customers and employees, you don't have any warning signs—but that still doesn't mean you can set it and forget it.

Staying vigilant and dealing with reality using your positive relationship with feedback helps you to understand why things are working or not. Just because you like the answers doesn't mean things are perfect. Check to see if the measurements are accurate. Ask, "Do the measurements reflect reality?" and "What are we not measuring?"

Finally, as a human being in a stressful position, make sure that you yourself are functioning well and not sliding to the right. Know yourself by asking what is essential to your well-being. Have a healthy state of awareness. Find what works best for you.

If you are balanced, you are more open to feedback. Using that feedback helps you keep evaluating yourself and your business.

Transformation Is Not a Straight Line

In the front row of the chartered airplane, the head football coach cried into his hands. His assistant coaches gathered around him, shielding him so the players would not see their frustrated leader.

The team had just lost a close game—their eighth loss in a row. Earlier in the season, they had won their first three games and seemed to have finally turned the corner from their prior struggles. Now, the coach thought he might be fired.

On that late-night cross-country flight home, the coach had almost decided to resign when he started to think about his role on the team. Every person in the organization had a role—and a responsibility to perform that role at the highest level. He himself had made sure of it.

He couldn't abandon the team now.

Slowly, the coach regained his composure. He sat up, drank a glass of orange juice, and ate a few peanuts. Instead of writing his resignation, he started planning for the team's upcoming game in less than a week. By 3:00 a.m., when the airplane landed, he was realigned with his own Standard of Performance.

Bill Walsh recovered, and the 49ers won their next game. They finished the 1980 season 6–10. Walsh kept his job, and the next season his team went on to win the first Super Bowl in the 49ers' thirty-one-year history.

There will be times when you question how the transformation of your company is going. You may doubt whether the changes you're making are really working, and you might even consider quitting. When that happens, return to the answers you defined using your chosen core alignment tool. Those answers are not just for the benefit of the rest of the organization. They will help you as the leader through challenging moments, as well.

When you maintain alignment in your business, you have the power to achieve an uncommon advantage over the competition. And your chances of reaching your desired outcome rise beyond measure.

Now that you have learned how to climb a mountain and keep your balance at the top, the next chapter will show you how to build on that momentum as you find the next starting line.

Chapter 8

Find the Next Starting Line

Accelerate

"Alex, I want to sell this business in the next twelve to eighteen months."

Don was the owner of a health-care business. At the time, the industry was facing some real challenges. "Okay. How much do you want to sell it for?" I asked.

His answer was more than double what I thought the company was worth. And he wanted to do it in the space of a year?

If he gets half of that, he'll be really successful, I thought.

We talked about the reality of what the company was worth today and what type of growth would be necessary to support his valuation. Don's business was growing, but he needed to accelerate the growth and current pace of improvement. Fortunately, the business was already aligned—and Don was in the position to leverage that alignment.

And that's exactly what he did.

Don accelerated his improvement process. He challenged assumptions and how things were done. He realigned his sales process, commission structures, product offerings, and customer service. Every month, we analyzed what was working and what wasn't. We dug deeper into all aspects of the revenue cycle.

Fewer than eighteen months after that first conversation, Don called and invited me and my wife to a five-star luxury resort for a celebration weekend with his team. He had sold the company for more than his original goal.

Don leveraged his company's alignment to reach his goals. You can do the same.

When Endings Become Beginnings

Your business, like your life, is always changing. You never cross a finish line without discovering something exciting: that finish line is also the next starting line.

And when you work and live with a healthy relationship with feedback, you have the emotional energy and awareness to actively ask yourself where that next starting line is.

Is it internal? Is it external? What should your next project be? How can you add value for yourself, to those around you, and to the larger world?

One of the biggest "next starting lines" you can reach is realizing that you've achieved success with your current business, but that you yourself are ready to strive toward a new goal that better aligns with the answers to your essential questions.

As you grow, you will come up with all kinds of different business ideas. For a while, many of them may fall under the same umbrella as your first one. But the day may eventually come when your new ideas begin to form an alignment pyramid of their own, with a different core than your original business. When that day arrives, you can embrace a new era of personal and professional growth.

You have a healthy relationship with feedback. You understand how to align a business with its own set of blueprints.

You are ready for the next starting line.

The OODA Loop Advantage

In any business you undertake, once you and your team embrace and complete the alignment process, you will see the results. Things are different, the frustration is gone, and you can feel it.

You now have a great opportunity: the ability to accelerate the growth process and create an unstoppable force with your company.

When people in a company are on the same page, they can do things faster than unaligned companies can. Aligned companies can more quickly observe what is happening in their environments, decide how to deal with a changing reality, and take the best action to address it.

When a company can do this process quicker and more effectively than its competitors can, it develops a real competitive advantage. The process is called the OODA Loop.

The OODA Loop is an enhanced feedback loop. The acronym stands for Observe, Orient, Decide, and Act. It was coined by Colonel John Boyd, a famous US Air Force fighter pilot in the 1960s. Boyd was instinctively good as a fighter pilot before the Air Force knew how to really train fighter pilots, so they put him in charge of training other fighter pilots. He developed the OODA Loop by analyzing how fighter pilots could gain an advantage over the enemy. In practice, those who quickly and effectively used the OODA Loop had the advantage, while those who didn't were not likely to survive.

The OODA Loop says that the competitor who can more quickly observe and orient him- or herself to what is going on, decide what to do, and take action—while effectively repeating the process as the situation changes—has the advantage even if he or she is in an inferior initial position or inferior aircraft.

This stuff has been tested at the Darwin level, in combat environments. And it works for businesses, too.

Learning how to use the OODA Loop to create an advantage is the next starting line for an aligned business. It can accelerate growth and help you identify and deal with threats before they sink your business.

The Bigger Impact

The benefits of alignment don't stop with your business. They bleed into the rest of your life as well.

I experienced this personally. Years ago, I didn't live in alignment. I was frustrated a lot, and I didn't have a healthy relationship with feedback. Obstacles used to drive me crazy, and I was impatient.

I brought all those things home with me. Over the weekends, I'd stew on specific situations, or people who didn't embrace potential solutions. My wife and daughter were getting tired of my act. Finally, during one weekend of extreme frustration with one client, my wife asked me point-blank, "Isn't this the same as the last client, and the client before that?"

Which was her way of asking me, "Is the problem really the client, or is it you?"

I knew what her answer to that question was. And I also knew that she was probably right.

As I learned more about business alignment, I began implementing its key principles in my personal life. I started questioning whether the decisions I was making were aligned with what we valued as a family. Did the things we invested time and money in help us lead meaningful lives?

In a lot of cases, they didn't. And we ended up realigning a lot of stuff.

Our realignment started on a Sunday evening while I was closing the swimming pool cover. "Why do we have this pool?" I asked myself. It didn't bring value into our lives. Instead, it was a decorative burden. I asked my wife and daughter the same question. They agreed that it didn't add very much to our happiness.

Eventually, we started questioning everything. We sold our house and ditched the decorative burdens. My wife and daughter began to spend more time doing what they really loved—riding horses. I was able to spend more time on my hobbies of photography and writing.

We cut out what wasn't necessary and strove to align our lives with what brought us meaning and fulfillment. And I personally have never enjoyed living more. Now, I enjoy the challenges I seek out. There is no tension to bring home.

"I don't know who you are, but I truly enjoy being married to you," my wife told me one day. After more than seventeen years of marriage, I can tell you that that has not always been the case.

That's the power of living in alignment.

Where to Start

The number one question I hear from every client I work with is this: "Where do I start?"

The answer to that question depends on understanding where you're at. Now, you have the knowledge to begin to identify your personal starting line. If you already have a healthy relationship with feedback, you may be at the point where you're ready to choose a core alignment tool for your business. Most stuck leaders need to begin by improving their relationship with feedback.

Whatever the case, you don't need to embark on the journey of aligning your business alone. Plenty of business coaches have climbed this mountain before you, and partnering with the right one will accelerate your growth toward your finish line.

I myself have resources available to help you with starting on the road to alignment. Whether you need to improve your relationship with feedback, understand where your company is stuck, or locate a coach who is right for you, I can help to point you in the right direction. You can access free alignment resources and connect with me at www.BusinessAlignmentTools.com.

As long as you understand your unique challenges as you strive to cross the starting line, you will quickly gain confidence in your ability to break free of the circle of frustration once and for all. And once you start, you can keep pursuing the path to growth with remarkable results.

The Next Starting Line

When things finally align in your business and your life, it's a truly amazing feeling.

The experience of achieving alignment for a month, for a quarter, for a year and beyond is like hearing that perfect note of music. The frequency of that sound is never strained or abrasive. There's a purity and an ease to it that carries naturally through a space—like a reminder that this is the way it was meant to be all along.

When you embrace alignment, the struggle and stress of the daily grind finally come to an end. You no longer have to fight yourself, or the people around you.

Instead, you have harmony. And along with harmony comes freedom, and ultimately fulfillment.

If you have been stuck in frustration, I hope you now see that there is a way forward. There *is* a place to start, and you do have the power to embark on this path of harmony and alignment.

Define your personal core by asking essential questions and using the answers to make big and small decisions. Find the next starting line in your business and your life.

Then start transforming your company. And never look back.

WORKS CITED

Bloom, Robert. 2008. *The Inside Advantage: The Strategy That Unlocks the Hidden Growth in Your Business.* New York: McGraw Hill. Kindle edition.

Covey, Stephen R. 2009. *The 7 Habits of Highly Effective People.* New York: RosettaBooks. Kindle edition.

Gawande, Atul. 2009. *The Checklist Manifesto: How to Get Things Right.* New York: Metropolitan Books.

Gerber, Michael E. 1988. *The E-Myth: Why Most Businesses Don't Work and What to Do about It.* Pensacola, FL: Ballinger Publishing.

Goldratt, Eliyahu M. 2004. *The Goal: A Process of Ongoing Improvement.* 3rd rev. ed. Great Barrington, MA: North River Press. Kindle edition.

Harnish, Verne. 2002. *Mastering the Rockefeller Habits: What You Must Do to Increase the Value of Your Growing Firm.* New York: Select Books.

Harnish, Verne. 2014. *Scaling Up: How a Few Companies Make It...and Why the Rest Don't.* Ashburn, VA: Gazelles.

Kotter, John P. 2012. *Leading Change.* Boston: Harvard Business Review Press.

Lencioni, Patrick. 2002. *The Five Dysfunctions of a Team: A Leadership Fable*. San Francisco: Jossey-Bass.

Lencioni, Patrick M. 2012. *The Advantage: Why Organizational Health Trumps Everything Else in Business*. San Francisco: Jossey-Bass.

Searcy, Tom, and Barbara Weaver Smith. 2008. *Whale Hunting: How to Land Big Sales and Transform Your Company*. Hoboken, NJ: John Wiley & Sons.

Sinek, Simon. 2009. *Start with Why: How Great Leaders Inspire Everyone to Take Action*. New York: Penguin. Kindle edition.

Smart, Bradford D. 2012. *Topgrading: The Proven Hiring and Promoting Method That Turbocharges Company Performance*. 3rd ed. New York: Penguin. Kindle edition.

Stack, Jack. 1992. *The Great Game of Business*. New York: Doubleday.

Walsh, Bill, Steve Jamison, and Craig Walsh. 2009. *The Score Takes Care of Itself: My Philosophy of Leadership*. New York: Penguin. Kindle edition.

Warrillow, John. 2010. *Built to Sell: Creating a Business That Can Thrive without You*. Toronto, ON: Flip Jet Media.

Wickman, Gino. 2011. *Traction: Get a Grip on Your Business*. Expanded ed. Dallas, TX: BenBella Books.

ABOUT THE AUTHOR

Alex Vorobieff is the founder and CEO of The Alex Vorobieff Company, a premier business-transformation company. A highly sought-after speaker and business coach, Vorobieff has transformed scores of multi-million-dollar companies into unstoppable forces using "business alignment tools"—a term he coined after years of working with and investigating different business systems.

Vorobieff specializes in helping companies get their team members on the same page to achieve desired outcomes. Through his company, he assists frustrated leaders in finding their unique starting lines, selecting the best alignment tools for their specific situations, and finally achieving clarity from chaos in their businesses.

In addition to solving thorny business problems, Vorobieff enjoys pursuing his hobby of photography. He lives in Newport Beach, California, with his wife Christine; their daughter, Kate; and their two horses.

TRANSFORM *YOUR* COMPANY

Are you ready to transform your business?

The Alex Vorobieff Company (AVC) offers resources to help you escape frustration and start your journey on the road to business alignment. Learn to generate real returns on your business improvement projects by:

Saving time and money with a personalized Starting-Line Assessment

Improving your relationship with feedback to accelerate growth

Identifying the right business alignment tools to free you from frustration

Finding a coach who is right for you to achieve desired outcomes

AVC offers webinars, workshops, and one-on-one consulting to help you and your team make sense of your unique situation, so you can transform your business into an unstoppable force.

To access free business alignment resources, or to connect with Alex, contact The Alex Vorobieff Company at (949) 478-0042 or visit www.vorobieff.com.

www.ingramcontent.com/pod-product-compliance
Lightning Source LLC
Chambersburg PA
CBHW060614210326
41520CB00010B/1338